Problem-Based Approaches to Physics
Changing perspectives in higher education

IOP Series in Physics Education

The IOP Series in Physics Education aims to provide comprehensive, authoritative and innovative coverage for those that teach physics and related subjects at universities and other higher and further education institutions, and for those involved in physics education research.

Series Editor
Professor Peter Main
King's College London, UK

About the Editor
Peter Main obtained his PhD from the University of Manchester and, after postdocs in Manchester and Helsinki, he joined the University of Nottingham as a Lecturer in Physics in 1979. Following promotions to Reader and Professor, he eventually became Head of the School of Physics and Astronomy. His principal research interests were in quantum fluids and quantum transport in semiconductor and metallic heterostructures. He was also involved in many teaching innovations.

In 2002, he left Nottingham to join the Institute of Physics as Director of Education and Science. In this post, he had overall responsibility for the Institute's work in education at all age levels, research and diversity. Among many projects, he worked closely with Ofqual and awarding bodies on curriculum matters and with government to increase the number of physics teachers. He also initiated several projects improving the diversity of participation in physics.

In 2015, he joined King's College to become Head of Physics; he retains his interest in many projects in physics education and diversity.

About the Series
The IOP Series in Physics Education aims to provide comprehensive, authoritative and innovative coverage for those that teach physics and related subjects at universities and other higher and further education institutions, and for those involved in physics education research.

The series supports evidence-informed professional practice and will cover topics including: assessment methods; feedback; conceptual understanding; problem solving; teaching methods; education technology; pedagogical theory; curriculum design; student engagement; misconceptions; employability; and social aspects of education.

Authors are encouraged to take advantage of electronic publication through the use of colour, animations, video, data files and interactive elements, all of which offer particular benefits in communicating pedagogy.

Do you have an idea for a book you'd like to explore?
We are currently commissioning for the series; if you are interested in writing or editing a book please contact Caroline Mitchell at caroline.mitchell@ioppublishing.org.

Problem-Based Approaches to Physics

Changing perspectives in higher education

Derek Jeffrey Raine
Department of Physics and Astronomy, University of Leicester, Leicester, UK

IOP Publishing, Bristol, UK

© IOP Publishing Ltd 2020

All rights reserved. No part of this publication may be reproduced, stored in a retrieval system or transmitted in any form or by any means, electronic, mechanical, photocopying, recording or otherwise, without the prior permission of the publisher, or as expressly permitted by law or under terms agreed with the appropriate rights organization. Multiple copying is permitted in accordance with the terms of licences issued by the Copyright Licensing Agency, the Copyright Clearance Centre and other reproduction rights organizations.

Permission to make use of IOP Publishing content other than as set out above may be sought at permissions@ioppublishing.org.

Derek Jeffrey Raine has asserted his right to be identified as the author of this work in accordance with sections 77 and 78 of the Copyright, Designs and Patents Act 1988.

ISBN   978-0-7503-2224-9 (ebook)
ISBN   978-0-7503-2222-5 (print)
ISBN   978-0-7503-2223-2 (mobi)

DOI   10.1088/2053-2563/ab3803

Version: 20191001

IOP ebooks
ISSN 2053-2563 (online)
ISSN 2054-7315 (print)

British Library Cataloguing-in-Publication Data: A catalogue record for this book is available from the British Library.

Published by IOP Publishing, wholly owned by The Institute of Physics, London

IOP Publishing, Temple Circus, Temple Way, Bristol, BS1 6HG, UK

US Office: IOP Publishing, Inc., 190 North Independence Mall West, Suite 601, Philadelphia, PA 19106, USA

To Sothis

Contents

Preface	ix
Acknowledgements	xi
Author biography	xii

1 Teaching and learning in higher education — 1-1

1.1	The changing environment	1-1
1.2	Developments and drivers	1-4
1.3	Strategically important subjects	1-6
1.4	Supply side	1-7
1.5	Innovations in pedagogy	1-9
1.6	Excellence and curriculum design	1-12
1.7	Problem-based approaches	1-13
	References	1-14

2 The curriculum and design science — 2-1

2.1	How students learn	2-1
2.2	The learning cycle	2-4
2.3	Affective learning: motivation	2-6
2.4	History of problem-based approaches	2-7
2.5	Enquiry and collaboration	2-11
2.6	Research–teaching nexus	2-11
2.7	Technology	2-14
2.8	Constructive alignment: design science	2-15
2.9	Personalised curriculum	2-19
	References	2-20

3 Alignment — 3-1

3.1	Outcomes	3-1
3.2	Engagement	3-4
3.3	Metacognition	3-8
3.4	Formative and summative assessment	3-9
3.5	Authentic assessment	3-12
3.6	Authenticity and employability	3-15
	References	3-17

4 Implementing problem-based approaches — 4-1
4.1 What is a 'problem'? — 4-1
4.2 The learning cycle — 4-9
4.3 Scaffolding problem-based approaches — 4-10
4.4 Managing problem-based approaches: shapes and sizes — 4-11
4.5 Managing problem-based approaches: facilitation — 4-13
4.6 Managing problem-based approaches: groups — 4-14
4.7 Managing assessment and feedback — 4-15
4.8 Managing change — 4-17
4.9 Putting it together: an example — 4-18
References — 4-21

5 Problem-based physics (and other disciplines) — 5-1
5.1 Sources of problems — 5-1
5.2 Laboratory PBL — 5-10
5.3 Induction — 5-13
5.4 Other disciplines — 5-15
5.5 Management — 5-16
References — 5-18

6 Do problem-based approaches work? — 6-1
6.1 Results from active learning — 6-3
6.2 Meta-analyses of the impact of PBL — 6-4
6.3 Employers' views on graduate employability — 6-5
6.4 Buy-in from staff and senior management — 6-6
6.5 Problem-based approaches across cultures — 6-7
6.6 The future of problem-based pedagogies — 6-8
References — 6-9

7 Problem-based approaches: looking to the future — 7-1
7.1 Structural change: the teaching focussed lecturer — 7-1
7.2 Physics and society — 7-4
7.3 What is physics? — 7-6
7.4 Interdisciplinarity — 7-8
7.5 Personalised curricula — 7-9
7.6 Sustainability — 7-10
References — 7-11

Preface

This book is about changing *perspectives* and *changing* perspectives in higher education. By this, I mean that I shall discuss how I think the landscape of university education is changing, and how I think we need to adapt the way we teach in the context of those changes.

My argument will be that we should use problem-based pedagogies as the basis of programme design in higher education. To make this argument, I start, in chapter 1, with a brief review of the history of university education and considerations of what it is for. The focus is largely on the UK although, apart from the details, much of the discussion is recognisably of much wider applicability. Here, and throughout the book, I try to defend again the widely rehearsed argument that universities are not simply training grounds for commercial and industrial workers. The employability of graduates is a crucial factor, but it will be a natural consequence of an educational system that is focused on the wider preservation and creation of social capital.

In chapter 2, I explore the essential background to the way in which formal learning occurs in order to arrive at the reasons for problem-based approaches. I use this somewhat ungainly term to cover the range of pedagogies often referred to simply as problem-based learning or PBL. As explained in this chapter, the reason I do not use the term PBL for this spectrum is that I want to emphasise the range of pedagogies included in this book, so I reserve the PBL appellation for the original, so-called medical model of PBL. The range extends from pure PBL at one extreme (even less constrained by specific learning objectives than the medical model), through project-oriented PBL (which, with a focus on project work, is I think the most widely practiced form), through what I call problem-based tuition (which employs the teacher supported scaffolding of project-based work, but in more of a problem-oriented context) to flipped learning (which can be thought of as problem-based tuition without the problem wrapper). This book then is a polemic for general problem-based approaches that have been developed from the original idea of PBL.

In chapter 3, I set out the background to the implementation of problem-based approaches. The crucial point I want to make here is that we should be concerned with the alignment of the whole curriculum, not just the teaching in individual modules or courses. The other point here is the need to treat curriculum design as a design science, evaluated at each iteration not by student satisfaction ('happy sheets'), but by studies of student behaviour and evidence of learning. (I do not want satisfied students—I want them hungry for more.)

In chapter 4, I look at the principal components of problem-based approaches, and the many ways of implementing them in practice. This is intended as a guide, not an instruction manual for implementation (of which there are many). The illustrations draw largely on my experience in physics, although I have tried to make them generally accessible. In chapter 5, I am specifically concerned with the development of the problems for problem-based approaches in Science, Technology, Engineering and Mathematics, specifically in physics. My experience is that the creation of good problems is difficult, and requires a deep knowledge of the discipline. I would like to have sufficient expertise in the humanities and social sciences to make constructive suggestions in these areas, but regrettably I do not. I shall restrict myself to some brief remarks. However, the ways in which problems fail, which I discuss in this chapter, are less discipline specific and may be of wider interest.

Having established, at least as a working hypothesis, the theoretical superiority of problem-based pedagogies over traditional ('lecture-based') methods, in chapter 6 I look briefly at the vast array of evidence. Just to assemble and read a significant fraction of the meta-studies is a large undertaking (which I have not undertaken). Even so, there are relatively few examples of physics programmes taught by problem-based approaches or having a large problem-based component. I am, however, fairly confident with my conclusions here as to what the literature says: that problem-based pedagogies are definitely no worse than traditional methods for learning content, are better in many instances and that the difference appears to be related to the way in which problems are scaffolded; that problem-based approaches are probably significantly better for long-term recall; that these pedagogies are better at developing skills, including researching for knowledge and applying it; that they can deliver a net gain in student retention; and that more work is needed to study student behaviour in order to identify the specific aspects of these approaches in practice that promote learning, and why they sometimes fail.

Several academic journals are devoted to PBL (and related pedagogies): The *Interdisciplinary Journal of Problem-Based Learning* (https://docs.lib.purdue.edu/ijpbl/), the *Journal of Problem-Based Learning in Higher Education* (https://journals.aau.dk/index.php/pbl) and the *Journal of Problem-Based Learning* (https://www.ejpbl.org/). There is also a large literature in the general education journals. Problem repositories can be found on-line, although these are subject to the continuing willingness of their hosts to maintain them. One with the greatest longevity is the PBL Clearing House of the Institute for the Transformation of University Education at the University of Delaware (www1.udel.edu/inst/). The ITUE website also has links to other institutions. Example problems will also be available at the author's website https://derekraine.com/.

In chapter 7, I come back to what a university is for in the light of our previous discussion. How is it that we can bring together a vision of an industrial, technological society with a respect for the study of the philosophy of the ancient Greeks and new translations of Dante? I think we can answer this in terms of the contemporary zeitgeist of sustainability. If we believe that the world is worth sustaining, then we have a reason to preserve and create the requisite social capital. It is the educational system that makes this possible, and it is our responsibility to ensure that the approaches we use are, on the evidence, the most effective we can come up with.

Acknowledgements

I have benefitted from collaboration with many people in the development of problem-based approaches to programmes in Physics and in Natural Sciences at the University of Leicester and from many discussions with developers of problem-based innovations in numerous institutions elsewhere. Dr Sarah Symons (now at McMaster) was my project manager for several years in the FDTL4, CETL and Stimulating Physics programmes and this book is dedicated to her. She, along with Tania Ruiz, helped set up the Natural Sciences degree programme at Leicester. Together, we ran the annual LeAP summer workshop on PBL for a number of years, where we probably learned at least as much from the delegates as they did from us. On the laboratory side, Ray McErlean and Tom Preston rose to many challenges and provided invaluable help to our numerous summer interns. More recently, the team of Sarah Gretton, Dylan Williams, Cheryl Hurkett, Kath Clarke and Paul Abel have developed problem-based pedagogies for our Natural Sciences programme. On the administrative side, very little would have happened without the organisational skills of Norma Corby, Joan Collier, Naomi Banks, Merry Holmes and particularly Alex Mack.

The team at the University of Delaware, George Watson in particular, provided invaluable advice in getting us started in PBL, and we had help from Brian Bowe at DIT, Maggie Savin-Baden at Coventry University and Ranald Macdonald at Sheffield Hallam. Finally, from a very long list of cheer-leaders for our development of problem-based pedagogies, I would like to thank Bob Lambourne, who led piCETL at the Open University, and Peter Main and Philip Diamond for their support during their time at the Institute of Physics.

Much of the development work was funded through grants from HEfCE (through FDTL4 and CETL) and in collaboration with IOP (Stimulating Physics) as well as small grants from the University of Leicester and the Higher Education Academy Physical Sciences Subject Centre.

Author biography

Derek Jeffrey Raine

Derek Jeffrey Raine is Emeritus Professor in the Department of Physics and Astronomy at the University of Leicester. He has led several major projects developing problem-based approaches in Physics and founded the Natural Sciences programme at Leicester, an interdisciplinary programme delivered by problem-based tuition. He was awarded the Bragg Medal of the Insitute of Physics for his work on curriculum development through problem-based learning, and an MBE for services to science education. He is a National Teaching Fellow and a Principal Fellow of Advance HE. In 2017, the Natural Sciences teaching team at Leicester won a CATE award from the Higher Education Academy for their work on embedding employability. He currently chairs the IOP Higher Education Advisory Committee and is a co-chair of the national Society for Natural Sciences, which he helped to set up.

IOP Publishing

Problem-Based Approaches to Physics
Changing perspectives in higher education
Derek Jeffrey Raine

Chapter 1

Teaching and learning in higher education

1.1 The changing environment

In the year 1600, just over one per cent of the population of England, in the relevant age group, went to university (all men, of course). They had a choice of either Oxford or Cambridge. In 1930, a little over 300 years later, just over one percent of the relevant age group (now only mostly male) went to university. They had a wider choice of 11 other universities [1]. In 2018, 33% of 18 year olds (slightly more women than men) were accepted into higher education (not quite the same as attending a university, but close enough to indicate the trend) [2]. This expansion of higher education began after the First World War and has accelerated since the Second World War. There is a paradox here. Prior to the First World War, universities were predominantly teaching institutions with less of a focus on original research. Only after that war, and more intensively after the Second World War, there was a shift to research. This was driven, predominately in the sciences, partly by the Cold War and partly by the recognition of the impact of scientifically based technology on economic growth. Thus, much of the great expansion in university education in England occurred in institutions that were no longer focussed on education, except in one regard: as elitist institutions selecting for new generations of academic researchers.

Thus, students who failed to show an aptitude for academic research were, somehow by default, deemed to have had adequate preparation for employment outside academia. The granting of university status in 1992 in the UK to the then polytechnics and technical colleges intended to address, to some extent, this strange state of affairs. This appears not to have worked out as envisioned, at least initially, as many of these new universities eagerly set out to establish research reputations. Such eagerness is well founded on the grounds that research reputation attracts good students who, with a small amount of guidance, can largely be trusted to educate themselves with (one hopes) little negative impact on research programmes. Furthermore, a reputation for research is both objective and visible, whereas, so the argument runs, good teaching is hard to define and still harder to discern, and, naturally, can anyway be effective only with good students. Much subsequent government policy seems to have been directed towards addressing these unintended consequences.

The UK is not alone in this move from an elitist structure of higher education to a mass system. The percentage of the population of advanced economies with university degrees in 2008 ranged between 49% (Canada) and 14% (Italy) [3]. Progress in some developing countries has been dramatic. Overall, 6.7% of the world population have a degree, rising by 0.78 percentage points per year. This is not simply an expansion through 'more of the same'. There is a feedback loop between the drivers of participation and the outcomes. In the 14th century, Bologna students entered that first university to equip themselves for medical or legal careers and would pay according to the effectiveness of their teachers. In Victorian England, a university education (at either Oxford or Cambridge) prepared graduates for the Church, or failing that, for a role in Imperial government. It was the ensuing laxity of standards that brought about government action to reform the two English universities. Various drivers have been proposed for the current expansion, including a growing middle class and social aspirations [4], and the expansion of technical and professional employments. In the change from an elite to a mass system, any or all of these drivers change the nature of the university.

In the early stages of the current expansion in the UK, attempts were made to develop teaching efficacy through staff training. This concentrated largely on advice on how to give a lecture, directed to researchers whose customary mode of presentation was little more than talking to themselves. Thus, we were encouraged to break up lectures with the occasional question to the audience, to which, in the ensuing silence, one would then provide the answer and move on. In some cases, lecturers would hand out printed notes with gaps. The notes were supposed to ease notetaking, and the gaps were intended to encourage attention (or attendance?). This meant students now had to simultaneously listen, read the blackboard, read the notes and write. In mathematical sciences, optional problem sheets were another innovation. In some institutions, today evolution is frozen at this point: lectures and optional problem sheets are the main delivery mode of the core material.

More recently in England and Wales, and in other domains that have been influenced by developments there (including Scotland which has its own system of education), the changes induced by the transition to a mass system can be summarised as 'accountability'. What universities are currently accountable for can vary depending on the government ministry or public body, but in the context of teaching it includes 'employability', 'accessibility', 'student satisfaction' and 'value for money'. The problem is that these are all both ill-defined and obviously unobjectionable. No-one is going to argue that universities should not give value for money or should exclude students on the grounds of social class (at least in a liberal democracy) or the associated lack of prior opportunities; no-one will argue that graduates should be unemployable. So, these all appear to be worthy outcomes. But, how should we operationalise them? How shall we measure them? Employability is not measured by the numbers of graduates in employment. Relativistic astrophysics is 'accessible' in a three-year degree programme to only a tiny minority of the population who have been adequately prepared. Can student satisfaction be measured at a single point in time, and does it give any meaningful indication of effective learning? Worst of all, value-for-money is not measured in terms of contact hours.

So, should our reaction be to person the barricades, defend the status quo or continue to tinker at the margins? I have been told more than once, by academics who have 'been teaching physics for many years', that they have no need of my telling them 'how to do it'. But, it is not the purpose of this book to tell people how to change their teaching. What I would like to do is to look at the design of the curriculum, and at approaches to pedagogy, in the light of the changing position of the university and of our growing knowledge of how learning works. I want to ask how we might interpret such ambitions as 'employability' and 'accessibility' in the context of a discipline and incorporate these into the design of the curriculum as a whole. While the discipline reference will be to physics, because that is my background, I have very little doubt that much of the discussion can be transplanted *mutatis mutandis* to most other disciplines. (Indeed, much of what I will discuss has been adapted *from* other disciplines.) In general, the reader can substitute their preferred discipline for 'physics'. I shall be explicit where I think this is not necessarily the case.

Here are a few quick examples, which we shall expand on later. First, on inclusivity: I am not responsible for the fact that physics has almost exclusively been developed by white males from Europe and its Western offshoots. I should be aware, however, that this is not a result of superior aptitude, but of historically greater opportunity. This suggests that my curriculum as a whole should be designed not to over-emphasise the glorious discoveries of past heroes, or, worse, not to attempt to rewrite that history, but to focus on the opportunities that this accumulation of knowledge presents to current students in the future.

Second, to address employability, it is not necessary to dilute the curriculum, but only to reorient it somewhat. We shall find that the relevant graduate attributes can all be interpreted in terms of the role of the professional physicist and ought therefore to be part of the curriculum design, without re-purposing the degree to a mere workforce training programme. As a specific example, as an external examiner, I have come across instances where modules have in general an average of let us say 60% and half of the students do not achieve much more than that. But, one module, in computing or a laboratory project, has an average of, say, 90% and most students perform excellently. The staff then scurry around to rescale the marks for this module or promise to make the module more difficult next year. Why? Programmes should cater for a range of student aptitudes. How does it help employability if some students never experience what it feels like to be an expert in something, never to have done something really well? How can students fulfil their potential if they never experience their potential, but only their limitations?

These are not issues of individual good teaching. They are issues of curriculum or programme design.

1.2 Developments and drivers

The previous paragraphs may give the impression that I think that curricula in general, and the physics curriculum in particular, have remained unchanged despite the changing environment. This is not the case. We have had numerous initiatives over the past 40 years, and I will outline some of these later. But, then why, after 40 years, are we still talking about the issues?

To understand what has not changed in this discussion, let us look first at what has changed, beginning with the student cohort. The number of graduates obtaining first degrees in the UK increased by a factor of around five between 1970 and 2010, while the general population grew by about 20%. For much of this time, the number of physics graduates remained fairly constant. Then, over the period 1994–2016 the increase in entrants to physics was 65% against a general increase of 47% (UK first degree, full time). In any case, unless one believes that physics has attracted only the highest attaining students from other disciplines in recent years, it is clear that the range of ability of entrants to physics degrees is now wider than it was in the past. For most subjects, if not all, this is manifestly the case, even if one argues that widening participation has opened opportunities for more students to demonstrate their greater potential for higher education. In other words, while physics may be capturing a wider pool of highly qualified and talented candidates, that is unlikely to be the only source of increasing numbers.

Second, the nature of graduate employment has changed, with a wider range of employments becoming graduate entry jobs [5, 6]. These jobs may put the emphasis on a rather different set of graduate attributes, and the change may render gaps in graduate employability more visible. Some people argue that we should reverse this trend and return to a more elitist role for the university sector [7]. For the moment that argument has no traction, nor, in my view should it. But, these changes do mean that the university has to adapt to the new reality.

The third development is that the skillset demanded of graduates even within the same employments has changed. This is most obvious in the context of technology. My time as an undergraduate coincided with the development of one of the first virtual memory electronic computers, the ATLAS machine at Cambridge. There was no intimation that this would develop into a general-purpose machine that would run more than just numerical algorithms for solving equations. Now, of course, computers are part of the environment. However, the apparent ready availability of information provided by the Internet is illusory without the background knowledge to access this information reliably. So, the learning of core discipline knowledge is as important as ever in higher education. What has changed is what can be done with that core discipline knowledge through the access it provides to higher learning; this will impact professional employment and, as I will show, can be reflected in our pedagogy to advantage.

Finally, we should note that the landscape has changed, not only in relation to industry and commerce, but also in academic research. In most disciplines, the picture of the professor in the ivory tower is no longer apt (if it ever was). Academics need to work together, argue for resources and manage these, be entrepreneurial and explain (and perhaps justify) their research to the wider public. These are either exactly, or closely related to, the skills that are asked for by employers outside academia [8]. Embedded in the undergraduate curriculum, they will equip graduates for employment in both academic research *and* in the wider world.

These changes help to explain that the lack of graduate skills, decried by contemporary employers, is not the same deficit that was being complained about 40 years ago. The skills are more relevant and more challenging. In a sense, employers' wishes will always be unsatisfied: a new graduate cannot, by definition, have the aptitudes that come only with extensive workplace experience. But that said, I think there is a reason that the university sector does not do better. It is that in many programmes, 'skills' come as bolt-on extras, often as single-shot exercises. A single group activity, a presentation, a debate do not suffice to give graduates skills in team-working, pitching or negotiating. These skills need to be embedded in programmes. They need to be part of what it means to become expert *in the discipline*. My comments on professionalism in the previous paragraph should be sufficient to explain why I do not see this as problematic. We shall return to this.

The other external driver I want to mention here is usually presented under the heading of conceptual understanding, or lack thereof. The majority of work that has been done on this in physics comes from the USA. It involves surveys of general courses in physics given to students who will mainly not be physics majors. It is therefore not obviously relevant to programmes in the UK, which require students to study a single main discipline from the start of their university career. Nevertheless, what it shows is how hard it is to counter students' misconceptions; students are prone to maintain these outside the classroom even when they give the 'right answers' within the classroom. The remaining evidence in the UK is anecdotal. It comes from reports of interviews with applicants for teacher training positions and from on-line forums for teachers. Here are a couple of examples that I think are accessible to non-physicist readers, and which should illustrate the complexity of the issue.

We know that light travels at a constant speed and that it can be considered as a stream of particle-like entities called photons. Consider a photon that hits a reflecting surface. Since the velocity of the photon is reversed it must slow down, stop and speed up in the return direction. This contradicts the constancy of the speed of light. While you are thinking about that, here is another one. We know that bodies of different mass fall with equal acceleration under gravity in a vacuum. But, in the presence of air resistance, do spheres of identical radius but different mass (made of material of different density) fall with equal speed under gravity? Now, would we expect a new graduate faced with these questions to be able to respond immediately? (Indeed, would we expect all experienced physicists to do so?)

The answer to the first question is quite complicated and is not really spelt out in the standard physics curriculum. The most we should expect, I think, is that a graduate should be able to go away and look up the 'interaction of radiation with matter' and perhaps find the answer. (If you are interested, the incoming photon is absorbed by electrons in the reflecting material which then emits a new photon. Neither photon travels in free space at other than the speed of light.) The second question is also hard because the natural thought pattern is this: in a vacuum, both spheres fall with equal acceleration (hence with the same speed); the air resistance on each is the same at any speed because they have the same profile. Therefore (incorrectly) they fall with the same speed. To see this is wrong, we have to understand that bodies in a vacuum fall at the same rate because the mass cancels out of the equation of motion, so the motion cannot depend on the mass. When we add the extra force from air resistance, which does not depend on mass, this means that the mass no longer cancels from the equation. (The heavier one wins.) I might expect a new physics graduate to write down the equation and work through to the solution, but not necessarily on the spot in their head.

My point is not that conceptual understanding at this level is not important, but that, like employability, the way to think about conceptual issues comes with experience. Whether we can provide sufficient such experience in a three or four year first-degree programme, without sacrificing the core knowledge that I have just argued is also essential, is open to debate. But, to my mind, it is a valid ambition that our graduates should be able to address such conceptual problems and that our future teachers in particular should understand, as deeply as possible, what it is they are teaching beyond 'the facts'. Such understanding is not, I would argue, provided by traditional pedagogies that rely on lectures and problem sheets.

To summarise then, we are subject to a changing environment from the changing student cohort, from changing employability skills and from the need to produce graduates who understand what they have been taught well enough not just to restate it, but to make use of it in novel contexts.

1.3 Strategically important subjects

The disciplines of Science, Technology, Engineering and Mathematics (STEM) are labelled by the government as strategically important to the UK. What the government means is that these subjects produce too few suitably qualified graduates relative to the perceived needs of the economy. Indeed, a 2008 report from the IOP claimed that it is impossible to overproduce physics graduates, although the report also notes that this is partly because of the adaptability of physics graduates to non-physics roles [9]. This adaptability (if it is indeed present) comes at a cost, since STEM graduates are more expensive to produce than humanities graduates. In fact, the opposite argument has it that the employment of around half of physics graduates in non-physics roles is evidence that we already overproduce such graduates. It would follow that increasing the throughput in this pipeline is a very inefficient way of satisfying the needs of the economy. Willetts [1] has argued that if there were truly a need for more physics graduates their salaries would be higher.

One area where we know for certain that there is a shortage of graduates is in specialist physics teachers. This is a role which graduates either find unattractive or one for which they feel ill-equipped, either from their knowledge of what school was like for them, or from the lack of relevant experience at university. We shall return to the impact of the school experience in the next section.

If we agree that there is an unmet demand for physics graduates, either now or in the future, we have two options, not necessarily exclusive. The first is to increase demand. Initiatives to increase the flow of physics graduates have had some success. While the proportion of physics graduates as a fraction of the total declined between 2000 and 2008 even as the actual numbers held steady, there has been a significant increase since then, as we saw above. In particular, measures to widen access to under-represented cohorts have shown modest but positive results. Nevertheless, we should be aware that there is still an attainment gap between these under-represented cohorts and the wider student body.

Could it be not only that we need to stimulate demand, but that we need to look to the second of these options, at the supply side: are degrees in physics, as now presented, sufficiently attractive? Can we look to improve the attainment of students, so that a higher proportion is qualified for, and want to be employed in, highly skilled STEM jobs? And actually, even if there were no external motivators, should we not look at this supply-side aspect anyway, to see how it might be possible to enhance the student experience?

1.4 Supply side

So, let us look at the supply side: what is taught and how.

> After instruction, students, on average, are found to be less expert-like in their thinking than before. They see physics as less connected to the real world, less interesting, and more as something to be memorized without understanding. This is true in almost all courses, including those with teaching practices that have substantially improved conceptual mastery [10].

The Colorado Learning Attitudes to Science Survey (CLASS, pronounced C-LASS) looks at the extent to which students become more expert-like in their thinking after instruction in physics. (It has also been extended to other sciences.) One might argue that the survey has been deployed mainly in general undergraduate courses in the USA, which comprise few physics majors, and is therefore does not reflect the undergraduate experience in the UK. The survey instrument has also been subject to criticism [11]. However, this is to miss the point. What the survey is telling us is that the physics curriculum acts as a filter for only the most dedicated students. The survey has traction because it accords with our casual experience that many students are put off physics at school, and at university, even after they have chosen to study it.

Why might this be? I would suggest that to study physics, as it is taught, is amongst the most exacting tests of delayed gratification. There is so much learning of basic concepts in order to understand more basic concepts that the final revelation of the structure of the physical world, in the form of a problem sheet on differential manifolds and another on states in Hilbert space (mutually incompatible descriptions for the foreseeable future), comes as something of a let-down to many students.

This is even exacerbated by outreach lectures that tell us how exciting physics is by giving away the punch lines. Why do I need to go through the hard work of learning physics if I have just been told the answers?—unless, of course, I want to become an academic researcher to investigate the questions that have not been answered, and have the talent to do so. In fact, the false prospectus for physics, coupled with the one-off opportunity for higher education, risks drawing in students for whom the only option is then to develop a survival strategy. Let me give two examples.

One year 3 student came to my office to ask a question purportedly about the momentum representation in quantum mechanics. After some probing as to what it was the student did not understand, we got to an admission of the origin of the problem. This student had survived almost to the end of their formal education in physics, getting quite acceptable grades, without understanding what the notation for a function, $f(x)$, meant. How is this possible? Diligently the student had learned, where necessary, what to write and when to write it, without any insight. This is not an isolated case. My second example is of an examination script of a student working through a complex calculation on time-dependent perturbation theory. The answer breaks off at one point with the annotation 'sorry, I can't remember what comes here' and then continues with the correct calculation having skipped a few lines. For the examination, the student had clearly just attempted to learn by rote the sequences of symbols, as if this were a perfectly normal expectation.

Now, of course, this is anecdote and not evidence. But, does it not point to a possible supply-side problem? Some delayed gratification is part of the training for any professional qualification, but it needs both the delay and the gratification. Students need to see the pay-off in terms of their interaction with the world beyond the lecture room and examination hall.

What might the pay-off be? Let me start with some things that it is not. It is not some modern content like relativity or chaos theory in year 1 as a taster. It is not research stars talking about their work in introductory programmes. Nor is it applications of physics in current research, which are usually too advanced to be accessible, so just become more of the same. All of these are perfectly laudable, but they do not address the particular issue. They are cosmetic distractions from the core learning.

The development of expertise needs almost endless practice. That practice involves doing, not just watching. Doing involves not just practicing skills, but deploying them in the professional context. All activities, other than the traditional pedagogy in higher education, provide opportunities for participation. In games, in sport, in craft, in art, in drama, in music, students are provided with carefully calibrated experiences appropriate to their stage of learning. One might argue that laboratory practicals in science fulfil this role. But, they do not if they consist in closely following a script: this is just practicing physical skills.

All of this suggests we need a participatory pedagogy—a student-centred approach to learning. This requires us to look at what we teach, the order in which we teach it, the context in which we teach it and the way in which we teach it.

In the next chapter, I shall support this conclusion by looking at evidence for the way in which students learn. Much of this has been known for a century and has influenced approaches to the earlier stages of education. In the rest of the book, I shall look at ways in which we can implement such insights in higher education. In the final chapter, I will also present arguments for changing what we teach.

I have, as warned, tied much of the discussion to physics. Do other disciplines have a comparable problem? In many cases probably not to the same extent. The apparent difficulty with physics appears to be the heavy reliance on a symbolic description of the world which is literal rather than metaphorical. 'Electron' is not a metaphor, but a sign or symbol for a complex entity that appears to us in experiments (with wires, beams, diffraction and so on), pictures (waves or particles or vacuum excitations as required) and mathematics (Newtonian particle, relativistic particle, solution of the Dirac equation, as required). Other disciplines that capture abstract concepts in mathematical terms probably have similar difficulties to physics. Chemistry is an obvious example, but I am also thinking of psychology, economics and sociology and of course mathematics itself. That is not to say that the traditional lecture course is a good way for students to study other disciplines, but in chapter 3 I will explain why some disciplines might be more easily adapted to student-centred learning than others.

1.5 Innovations in pedagogy

I commented above that pedagogy in higher education was not static: there have been changes in most disciplines in various institutions in the UK and across the world. In physics, developments in research have fed into course content across the sector, usually as optional modules. These include not only discoveries in existing sub-disciplines, but also whole new sub-disciplines such as photonics, soft matter, quantum computing, biophysics, environmental physics, econophysics and even sociophysics. Researchers have no problem with bringing their discipline research into the undergraduate curriculum.

Educational research seems to fare less well. When I started teaching, lectures, problem sheets and scripted laboratories were the way things were done. There were attempts to make lectures more interactive, but these were largely met with passive hostility by students, and sometimes also by the staff who were supposed to implement them. Tutorials were largely general chats. Research projects for final year undergraduates were something of a novelty. Such projects are now universal in physics. Most curricula also include a group project. Workshops for problem-solving are also fairly common. There have been various experiments with research-based learning, the Keller plan, flipped learning, problem- and project-based learning, the use of simulations, trials of spaced repetition and various attempts to move away from scripted practicals. Assessment techniques have also expanded somewhat from 'do N out of M questions in T hours' to graded question sets and some continuous assessment of problem-solving. Doing a presentation of some sort is ubiquitous. Some authenticity is evident in the format of research reports, for example, where these are written up in the style of a journal article. Most practical sessions now require students to undertake some pre-laboratory preparation. This aims to reduce the cognitive overload of trying to combine technical skills and new physics, which underlay passive menu-driven approaches [12]. Numerous conference presentations each year present a variety of novel (and not so novel) interventions to improve student learning.

However, these developments have been largely piecemeal. It is not that teaching in universities is not better than it was 40 years ago. The issue is whether it is as good as it could be—whether indeed it is fit for purpose. One is reminded of the adage that no amount of tinkering will turn a horse into an automobile.

In the 1990s the first steps were made to recognise that changes in teaching practice required funding. This led to the introduction of relatively quite small institutional grants for teaching development. In theory, this allowed for the buy-out of some staff time, which could then be used to develop new approaches. As an example, one such grant funded my own initial pilot of a problem-based learning (PBL) activity. But, attempts to fund change have been largely time-limited and project-based. Problems with many of these initiatives included sustainability once funding ended (despite the continuation strategy incorporated into the project bid), and a dependence on individuals, which is lost once people move job roles or institutions. Because these interventions were largely unevaluated (apart from 'happy sheets') and unpublished outside the institution (because there was no reward for spending the additional effort, and nowhere to publish anyway), this has led to a lot of re-invention. Even now I sometimes listen to conference presentations of supposedly novel interventions that were new 30 years ago.

As far as resources for educational development for university physics is concerned, the physics discipline network was funded from 1994 by the then DfEE and brought together a small number of educational innovators. The DfEE also provided small grants, but the impact of these suffered the issues noted in the previous paragraph.

The LTSN Subject Discipline Networks, founded in 2000, represented an attempt on a national scale to address these negative aspects of local funding. The networks offered small grants to address issues that were of more than local relevance and encouraged collaboration. As well as national conferences and topic meetings, the Networks ran journals for dissemination of action research. Some of the published work might not have met the criteria for acceptance in the established educational research journals, but did serve to keep practitioners informed. The Networks were absorbed into the Higher Education Academy as the Subject Centres, which continued with this work until closed down in 2011 to save costs. Some of the activities continue as voluntary initiatives. In the physical sciences, this includes the journal [13] and the annual VICE-PHEC conferences.

A problem with small-scale funding is that it can only support small-scale initiatives, which are usually quite disparate; this approach therefore runs the risk that the total is less than the sum of parts. The first large scale national initiative in the UK was the series of projects under the auspices of the Fund for Development of Teaching and Learning (FDTL). These followed a national evaluation of every university department called Subject Review, a hugely costly exercise involving departmental visits by teams of six reviewers spread over three days. The methodology involved judgements of the outcomes against the department's own objectives. As the process continued over two years, departments became increasingly adept at matching their declared objectives to their evidence, thereby producing an early example of grade inflation. Access to FDTL funding was then open only to the top-scoring departments and had to involve cross-institutional collaboration. An interesting feature of this programme was an attempt to widen the impact by providing follow-on funding for other institutions to adopt the project outcomes. In our case, this aspect was not a success—not that there was no impact outside the project, but that has come many years down the line once some of the ideas have had time to percolate, not in immediate proximity. Implementing change in higher education has a long lead-in time.

An attempt to address the issues of scale and timescale was made in the next major national initiative, the Centres of Excellence in Teaching and Learning (CETLs—pronounced variously with a soft or hard 'C'). The idea was that these would be funded initially by special grants, but that institutions would take over running them once the initial funding ended. The funds included large capital grants, so that CETLs would have a visible (and presumably therefore continuing) presence. It may have had the opposite effect. While the Subject Centres were physically located on a particular campus, their physical presence in the host institutions was largely invisible, and hence of limited added value to the host. Working with them therefore did not feel like aiding the competition. I suspect that the same could not be said of the CETLs. It is also widely (if unofficially) agreed that the capital funding could have been better spent over a longer period.

The next idea for gaining impact, at least in STEM subjects, was to involve the professional bodies, which clearly have a national profile and established routes to dissemination. Initiatives have included Stimulating Physics and Chemistry for Our Future, which were followed by a national STEM programme [14]. Various programmes have addressed accessibility [15, 16].

The age of austerity then brought funding in the UK to a halt.

Nevertheless, why after millions of pounds spent and thousands of hours invested, does it seem like there is still a problem? That, to quote '…there is lamentable teaching that must be driven out of our system' [17]. There are three barriers to diffusion of good practice. One is the not-invented-here effect. What is good practice in one context may be genuinely unworkable in another. Or it may be that ownership of teaching is important for good delivery. Another problem, as I have already mentioned, is that innovation is unlikely to diffuse unless there is funding. The most important might be that it is not broken, we do not need to fix it. Thus, the argument goes, to initiate the change we must show that the system is not fit for purpose (while at the same time maintaining income from foreign students). Showing that the system is not fully functional seems to have become a government mission. So, what is actually wrong and how do we fix it?

1.6 Excellence and curriculum design

Professor Plonk gives lectures of model clarity in measured tones. His notes are complete and cover all the material exactly as it will be assessed. Professor Plonk gets excellent examination scores and student evaluations. But, none of the class thinks his subject is interesting. Professor Flybutter allows his enthusiasm to overcome his sense of organisation, He writes 'x' on the board, says 'y' and really means 'p'. But, his palpable love of the subject encourages his students to work at the material on their own, using the references in the library or on-line. Professor Flybutter gets rather mixed evaluations. Which is the good teacher? Well, we might ask before deciding, what were the examination results for Professor Flybutter? Or is that really all that matters? Should we perhaps suggest that some staff development might be effective? Because the truth is that we need instructors to communicate both content and enthusiasm—to motivate and to provide access.

There are a plethora of texts that provide evidence-based approaches to good teaching in higher education. Each tends to emphasise different aspects. Biggs [18] has constructive alignment, Ambrose et al [19] have research-based principles for smart teaching, Evans [20] focusses on a learning styles analysis, Laurillard [21] works on pedagogical patterns and Leamnson [22] tackles problems with the lecture format for unprepared first-year students. There are many others, probably mostly unread by most university lecturers. I do not intend to add to them through this book, because I think there is a different problem that needs fixing.

Plonk and Flybutter are pseudonyms for real academics who were world leaders in their research fields, recipients of prizes and awards for their work. Taking time away from what they can uniquely contribute to society, to work at something which others can do better, is not a good use of their rare talent. But, even suppose, we succeeded in developing their lecture styles, would this solve the problem? Does a succession of individually well-taught lecture courses prepare students for life outside academia? My argument in this book is that excellent teaching is more about the design of the curriculum as a whole than it is about individual excellence, whatever that might be. Excellent design will expose students to the different modes of learning and will use the individual contributors to teaching in roles that reflect their talents.

The educational system in the UK has many disadvantages: too early specialisation, a badly aligned university admissions system, and semesterisation superimposed on a disruptive term structure to mention a few. But, the system of higher education has one great advantage. In higher education in the UK, students are admitted to departments that determine the curriculum for their students. This gives academics overall control of the student experience. Students enter a programme, not a pick-and-mix smorgasbord. This programmatic approach is usually exploited to the extent that it allows control of the syllabus, so content can be efficiently sequenced. It should also give control of the development of the student as an independent learner, something which we singularly appear to fail to exploit. Students in the UK are efficiently educated, but not necessarily well-educated.

1.7 Problem-based approaches

To look more closely at appropriate curriculum design, we need to investigate the conditions under which students learn. We shall do this in some detail in the next chapter. To summarise here: in essence, we require a disposition to enquiry on the part of the student, and feedback to inform that enquiry through discussion and collaboration. Putting this together we arrive at some form of problem-based approach or problem-based pedagogy. (I shall use the terms interchangeably.) The problem, as a starting point, excites the disposition to enquiry and then provides a framework within which the learning can be achieved and against which it can be measured.

An elaboration of what I mean by a problem-based approach will be the subject of later chapters, but I should point out here that I mean something wider than, but including, what is normally referred to as PBL. Woods, one of the founders of PBL, identifies a matrix of options for student-centred learning depending on whether this is content- or problem-driven, and whether it is teacher-directed, teacher-guided or student directed [23]. Content-driven approaches can include student-directed group work and peer teaching. Woods includes case studies under teacher-directed, problem-based approaches. The traditional exercise set accompanying the lecture is content-driven, teacher directed and not problem-based, because the problems do not drive the instruction; they are used to check if it has been successful or to reinforce it. In Woods's characterisation, PBL is problem-driven and student directed.

Woods would, I think, argue that much of what I have to say in this book is not specifically about PBL (or about PBL at all), since the extent of student direction will be constrained more than the purist would allow. I do not see this as an issue. My purpose is not to sell a particular prescription, but to look at the range of reasons for implementing some form of problem-based approach and the ways of doing so. My experience is that this approach needs to be adapted to the discipline, and educational context, and supported accordingly. In particular, much of what I and my colleagues have implemented is perhaps closer to teacher-guided rather than student-led. If I were to invent a description for what we have developed, it would be problem-led tuition. I shall use this term later when I discuss our implementation. I shall refer to the whole class of pedagogies we are discussing as problem-based approaches (written in full). I shall distinguish the particular flavour that Woods describes by the acronym PBL (since this is how it is universally referenced), with the note that many authors use this term to encompass some or all of what we are calling problem-based pedagogies.

The use of the term problem-led tuition for our pedagogy has one obvious disadvantage in that it adds to what we shall see are the already large range of acronyms and descriptors for various problem-based approaches to learning. It has one advantage: it encapsulates not only the theoretical stance for the pedagogy, but also, in the term 'tuition', a practical methodology for implementation. There is a danger that the term tuition will be interpreted to mean just lecturing. The lecture has a place in tuition, but it cannot be the means by which the tutor discovers the progress that students are making with the problem. Thus, problem-led tuition cannot be achieved by the traditional mode of delivery; it requires dialogue with the students. In the UK, the term tutor and tutorial carry this implication of teaching as a two-way dialogue.

References

[1] Willetts D 2017 *A University Education* (Oxford: Oxford University Press)
[2] Patterns and Trends in UK Higher Education 2018 (https://www.universitiesuk.ac.uk/facts-and-stats/data-and-analysis/Documents/patterns-and-trends-in-uk-higher-education-2018.pdf)
[3] Education at a Glance 2010 OECD Indicators 2010 (http://www.oecd.org/education/skills-beyond-school/45926093.pdf) (table A1.3a)
[4] Trow M 1973 *Problems in the Transition from Elite to Mass Higher Education* (Berkeley, CA: Carnegie Commission on Higher Education) (https://files.eric.ed.gov/fulltext/ED091983.pdf)
[5] Green F and Henseke G 2014 The Changing Graduate labour Market: Analysis Using a New Indication of Graduate Jobs *LLAKES Research Paper No. 50* (https://www.llakes.ac.uk/sites/default/files/50.%20Green%20and%20Henseke_0.pdf)
[6] Chevalier A and Lindley J 2007 Over-education and skills of UK graduates *CEEDP* 79 (http://cee.lse.ac.uk/ceedps/ceedp79.pdf)
[7] Caplan B 2018 *The Case Against Education: Why the Education System is a Waste of Time and Money* (Princeton, NJ: Princeton University Press)
[8] Hanson S and Overton T 2010 Skills required by chemistry graduates and their development in degree programmes (Hull: HEA Physical Sciences Centre) (http://www.rsc.org/learn-chemistry/resources/business-skills-and-commercial-awareness-for-chemists/docs/skillsdoc1.pdf)
[9] Institute of Physics 2008 *Analysis on Demand for Stem Skills* (Institute of Physics response to a Department for Innovation, Universities and Skills consultation) (https://www.iop.org/policy/consultations/higher_education/file_41887.pdf)
[10] Adams W K, Perkins K K, Dubson M, Finkelstein N D and Wieman C E 2005 The design and validation of the colorado learning attitudes about science survey *AIP Conf. Proc.* **790** 45
[11] Douglas K A, Yale M S, Bennett D E, Haugan M P and Bryan L A 2014 Evaluation of Colorado learning attitudes about science survey *Phys. Rev. ST Phys. Educ. Res.* **10** 020128
Douglas K A, Yale M S, Bennett D E, Haugan M P and Bryan L A 2014 Evaluation of Colorado learning attitudes about science survey *Phys. Rev. ST Phys. Educ. Res.* **10** 029901 Erratum
[12] Johnstone A H, Watt A and Zaman T U 1998 The students' attitude and cognition change to a physics laboratory *Phys. Educ.* **33** 22–9
[13] New Directions in the Teaching of Physical Sciences 2019 (https://journals.le.ac.uk/ojs1/index.php/new-directions)
[14] Grove M 2013 National HE STEM Programme (https://www.birmingham.ac.uk/Documents/college-eps/college/stem/national-he-stem-programme-final-report.pdf)
[15] Institute of Physics 2000-09 *Stimulating Physics* (https://www.stem.org.uk/cx4t5)
[16] Royal Society of Chemistry 2009 *Chemistry for our Future* (https://www.nfer.ac.uk/media/1641/cff01.pdf)
[17] Johnson J 2015 Speech to universities UK (https://www.gov.uk/government/speeches/higher-education-fulfilling-our-potential) See the commentary by Mark Leach at https://wonkhe.com/blogs/how-to-read-jo-johnsons-speech-to-universities-uk/

[18] Biggs J and Tang C 2011 *Teaching for Quality Learning at University* (Berkshire: SRHE & Open University Press)
[19] Ambrose S, Bridges M, DiPietro M, Lovett M and Norman M 2010 *How Learning Works; 7 Research-Based Principles for Smart Teaching* (San Francisco, CA: Jossey-Bass)
[20] Waring M and Evans C 2015 *Understanding Pedagoy: Developing a Critical Approach to Teaching and Leaning* (London: Routledge)
[21] Laurillard D 2012 *Teaching as a design science: building pedagogical patterns for learning and technology* (New York: Routledge)
[22] Leamnson R 1999 *Thinking about teaching and learning: developing habits of learning with first year college and university students* (Sterling, VA: Stylus)
[23] Woods D R 1994 *Problem-Based Learning: How to Gain the Most from PBL* (Waterdown, ON: Donald R Woods)

IOP Publishing

Problem-Based Approaches to Physics
Changing perspectives in higher education
Derek Jeffrey Raine

Chapter 2

The curriculum and design science

Become such as you are, having learnt what this is [1].

In this chapter, I shall start by arguing that our knowledge of how students learn, both cognitively and affectively, leads us to design a problem-based approach to the curriculum. In the subsequent sections, I shall look at the evolution of problem-based pedagogies and how they address various aspects of curriculum design.

2.1 How students learn

From the point of view of physics, how the brain learns has an apparently simple answer: it is the process of reorganising the connections between neurons. The problem, however, is how to get the brain to alter those connections, since it is only through the existing connections that its connections can be affected. We cannot rewire the brain from the outside, but must persuade it to rewire itself. As a consequence, learning theories are not like theories in physics. Two different theories in physics in the same domain cannot both be right; one must supplant the other. (Of course, one theory may be derived from a deeper theory, but they would not then be different theories in the sense I mean here.) Our understanding of learning is quite different: alternative theories may supplement our understanding. That does not mean that all theories of learning have equal merit, but they may provide insights from different viewpoints. We need to understand many aspects of what goes on in the mind of the learner if we are to plan a curriculum that has any chance of promoting learning, other than by the rare accidental good fortune that we address students who need no teaching. In this section, I shall outline some basic ideas which will lead us to a problem-based approach.

The simplest description of learning dispenses with what is happening in the brain and just regards it as a device to connect an input to an output. This theory is called behaviourism [2]. It contends that we have learned something if we can operate in the world to produce a desired outcome. (This is to be distinguished from Pavlov's classical conditioning which just requires the correct response to a stimulus.) On this view, a teacher has simply to present learning tasks in an appropriate order, and the pupil has to practice each to the teacher's satisfaction before moving on to the next. A behaviourist would contend that we cannot examine the interior workings of another person's mind; all we can observe is their actions. Consequently, this is the only way we can evaluate learning.

The traditional approach to transmitting information to students has been called learning through acquisition. It is intended to go beyond behaviourism to examine what students can do with the supposedly acquired knowledge. There are various illustrations in the literature how learning by acquisition can become nothing more than behaviourist. Here is mine.

Students copy the following equations from the lecture:

$$\angle N = 0$$
$$\angle \wedge N = \nu_0 k$$
$$N = \nu_0 m P$$
$$G = \pi t^2 N$$

To show they have understood, they are presented with the following exercise:

Exercise: A long dparmpof of radius $t = 0.02$ m has $m = 10\,000$ yitmd m^{-1} and a vittrmy $P = 1$ amp. What is the zshmryov goraf N at its center? What is the gaic G through the dparmpof? (Take the constant ν_0 to be $\nu_0 = 4\pi \times 10^{-7}$ Henriettas m^{-1}.)

The problem is that you do not need any knowledge at all of the lecture content, or of physics in general, to do this: it is just pattern matching. (Try it; you can even almost get the units right even though you do not know what they mean!) The external feedback from the instructor does nothing to remedy this: the exercise will be marked as correct.

Learning by acquisition can be quite a difficult experience, akin to studying an instruction manual without knowing what the device is for, or even, without access to the device. A simple improvement would be to set the exercise in the context of some real-world consequence, which would provide some intrinsic feedback. This is not a foolproof solution. I have seen students who are apparently quite happy with results from substituting numbers in equations that make no sense: such things as negative atmospheric pressures and distances to the Moon of a few centimetres. There is also a multitude of examples from physics textbooks where supposedly real calculations use unrealistic values precisely because the numbers have not been made to matter—in other words, there is no intrinsic feedback [3]. However, setting a realistic context is at least one step towards engaging students with a problem if the context is something they might care about.

I think that most people would agree, for reasons we shall come to in a moment, that the behaviourist approach, and hence the closely related learning through acquisition, cannot be right. But, I have seen many teachers behave as if it is.

A student produces an erroneous calculation; the teacher hands out a correct calculation or writes it up on the board, which amounts to the same thing. The student makes an effort to learn the correct answer. If the question comes up in the examination, the student will be deemed to have learned the calculation if they can correctly reproduce it. But, what if a variant question is asked? How can the student adapt their behaviour if they do not have some mental model that constrains or suggests possible adaptations? So, behaviourism is not wrong—it is just not the whole story (or any great part of it). As Dewey [4] emphasised, formal education is about the propagation of what was created in the minds of our forebears to the minds of our successors. That we *do* have to get into the minds of others in order to teach effectively is what makes teaching so hard.

So, what is behaviourism missing? Accessing other minds requires social interaction and experience, that is, interaction with the social and material world. This is how children learn informally [5]. In formal education, the teacher is present to mediate and guide that interaction in order to ensure that it is within the students' capabilities. This is what Vygotsky [6] called the zone of proximal development. (There is some disagreement here on the extent to which learners need to be ready to learn and whether too modest a pace actually slows development [7], but this is no justification for the plough-on-regardless approach of the traditional lecture course.) While the research focus has been on the early stages of education, these observations on formal learning are valid at all stages. Dewey [8] emphasised the need for the teacher to create conditions under which the learner receives feedback from the environment (intrinsic feedback) as well as, as is usual in formal learning, from the teacher (extrinsic feedback). Learning in which the environment provides intrinsic feedback Dewey referred to as experiential learning.

The other thing that is missing—if we are to get into other people's minds—is an understanding of how people's minds work. This is the domain of cognitive neuroscience. In the early evolution of the discipline, the focus was on identifying common features of information processing. More recently, and more relevant to education, there have been attempts to articulate differences in the way people respond to the environment, and to correlate these with brain states. To give an example, cognitive scientists contrast the extent to which background context affects the perception of the foreground. They describe this as field-dependence versus field-independence. Other axes of difference that have entered the general consciousness are the intuitive-analytic distinction, the contrast between convergent versus divergent thinking and, of course, the now well-known difference between deep and surface learning.

Another distinction that has entered the arena as a way of exploring different learning approaches is VARK–which stands for visual, auditory, read/write and kinaesthetic. Unfortunately, this has led to the idea of preferred learning styles regarded as attributes rather than as adaptable strategies. (See [9] for a brief, excoriating review of learning styles as attributes.) Such learning styles are not fixed characteristics of a student to which the teaching has to adapt, as has been, and sometimes still is suggested. Learning styles are ways in which the student has to adapt to the material—with, of course, the teacher's help. The instructor should provide opportunities for multiple perspectives as appropriate to the content. (I think that kinaesthetics is perhaps under-utilised in physics education: imagining what it would be like to ride on a beam of light led Einstein to a Nobel prize.)

The creation of a mental model, that is the processing of information that takes us beyond randomised trial and error, requires the formation of concepts. These are essentially linguistic, both in form and in the way that they are transmitted. Vygotsky sees the role of language in 'word to thought and back' as essential for a systematic approach to the correction of error. Dewey emphasises the role of social interaction here: only the social world provides feedback for linguistic constructs.

For readers familiar with artificial neutral networks, an analogy might be useful. The association of output to input in a neural network is executed by some algorithm that adjusts the strengths of connections between the neurons of the network. This acts to diminish the error between the current output (which might be entirely random to start with) and the desired output for that input. The internal states of the network correspond in some way to a mental model of that linkage. The search algorithm ensures that the process of error correction is not random. The adjustment of the connections of the internal neurons (those not directly connected to input or output) is referred to as deep learning. In the real learner's brain, the algorithm itself is coded into the connection strengths. How this is achieved may in part be through hard wiring of the brain, and in part through the reflection on experience that we call metacognition. We shall return to metacognition (section 3.3).

2.2 The learning cycle

The problem of formal education is now easily stated. It is: How can we have an individual dialogue (error correction) in a system of mass education, that is, where, without one-to-one individual tuition, the instructor has only limited access to the errors she is trying to correct? We should be clear that the answer to this question is not to increase the number of hours students spend in class. To do this while conserving resources through larger classes would surely be counter-productive. An increase in contact hours, as conventionally envisaged for class teaching, and without changes to pedagogy, *reduces* the time available for individual learning. The current trend in the UK towards decreasing assessments in favour of increasing (or at least maintaining) class contact hours is retrograde in this regard, since it reduces the opportunities for individual feedback.

So, if the dialogue with the instructor is limited, then the feedback has to come from other parts of the learning environment. Thus, we need to think about framing the environment as a space for feedback. There are two aspects to this. We can use the physical environment to provide feedback. Papert [10] refers to this as constructionism. This might mean constructing a physical artefact, or it might mean interacting with a simulation. Such simulations may or may not be virtual. For example, a crime scene for teaching forensic science might be simulated physically or virtually.

Alternatively, the interaction could be with peers. Papert refers to this as constructivism. Such interactions require communication through the articulation of concepts, which is to say that they promote deep learning.

In either case then, the iterative feedback from the environment, and the on-going adaptation to the environment, promotes deep learning through the process of error correction. In both cases, the extrinsic feedback from the teacher is augmented by intrinsic feedback to the learner from the physical or social environment.

That these interactions are iterated brings us to learning cycles. There is a vast literature on these depending on how their authors link the cycle to various taxonomies of learning. So, let us start (very briefly) with taxonomies.

The idea is that we operationalise learning by describing what students do at various levels of development. These level descriptors constitute a taxonomy of learning. The most widely known is Bloom's taxonomy [11]. This has six levels ranging from recall to evaluation. Another popular way of organising progression is the SOLO taxonomy (Structured Observation of Learning Outcomes) [12] which, as its name suggests, is linked to the alignment of learning outcomes. The recall of a single idea is the second level in this taxonomy (the first is prestructural where the student has no idea at all) and the highest level (level 4) is using connected ideas about the subject to evaluate or predict.

The learning cycle is then a spiral [7] that takes the student round cycles of experience and error correction as they ascend the structural levels to create a mental model. Kolb's experiential cycle (figure 2.1) has gained a wide dissemination with variants [13].

One of the problems with the learning cycle, as it is currently implemented throughout higher education, is that students never get the chance to apply feedback

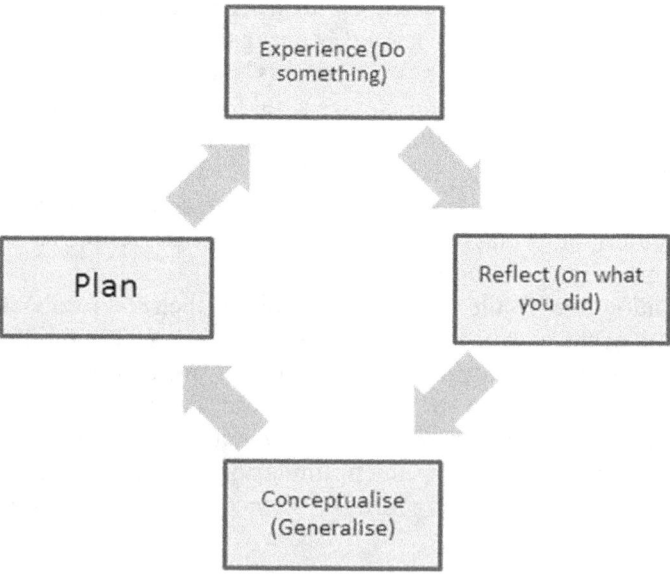

Figure 2.1. A learning cycle, based on [13].

in the same context as that in which they receive it. Instead, they are expected to exhibit what is a high-level skill in any taxonomy by adapting feedback received in one context to a continually changing one—a problem sheet on a quite different topic, an essay on a new subject with different forms of argument. Ambrose *et al* [14] give examples of how this fails to address student needs.

Many academics used to the ways of science get frustrated at this point because it seems that there are no laws of learning, but only different views jostling for attention. However, the important point for us is not the differences but the similarities. For that reason, I have not dwelt on the details of taxonomies and cycles, which are readily accessible in the references. Teachers may have an individual preference for how they label the levels of learning, or they may have no interest at all in how they are described. But, instructors do need to be aware of, and reflect on, how they are structuring what it is that they intend their students to do, and of the cycles of experience, they provide for the doing. It may well be that we want students to 'understand quantum mechanics', but we need to operationalise the process of understanding; that is, we have to say how we will structure the experiences that lead to understanding, and how we will measure progression through each of these experiences. In contrast to the experience of many academics, for most students, a mere suggestion of which textbook to consult (or a lecture course that repurposes the textbook in PowerPoint) may not be sufficient.

2.3 Affective learning: motivation

So far, we have dealt with the cognitive aspects of learning. However, the brain is not just a knowing organ but a feeling one too. Learning will not take place unless we attend to that aspect also. This leads us to the motivation for learning.

Even if materials and experiences are adequately structured, students nevertheless need to be motivated to learn. If the task is, say, to learn how to distribute a document electronically, then it might be sufficient to be told the requisite sequence of mouse clicks. There is no immediate payoff for attending to an explanation of how the server works in order that the learner might understand the sequence and be able to adapt it. For the somewhat more complex task of motivating study in higher education, in the past one might have held out the prospect of a research career. Nowadays the motivation is more likely to be the entry to a graduate job (however, that is defined) with a good degree (however, that is defined). Putting this together with the strong pressures in UK universities to eliminate drop-out rates, this has the potential for a downward spiral in standards. At least the ability to carry out academic research is to some extent objective. Graduateness and good degrees are largely convenient fictions, defined by the educational system—witness the increasing number of first-class degrees.

In any case, formal learning is oriented towards a goal. The goal might present itself at multiple levels. Let us use football (soccer) as an example (doubly appropriate as we are talking about goals). Suppose the student is learning to pass the ball, player to player. How would her practice lead to her doing this well if she does not know what she is trying to achieve? And how could she understand what she is trying to achieve except in the context of knowing the game. Some modicum of ability to pass the ball might be a first step, but we do not expect players to be technically expert before we let them take part in a game. If they are young players, we might adjust the dimensions of the pitch and the goal to suit their physiques, so we create a scale model of the professional game. I hope the metaphor in relation to academic learning is clear, except that the opponent in that case is Nature, and we do not so much seek to defeat her in the game as to elicit her secrets.

The task of learning therefore directs us to the solution of a problem, namely how to achieve the goal. One might suppose that we can approach the solution through a trial and error approach to experimentation. But, the notion that the association of reward with stimulus occurs through trial and error is untenable. It may work sometimes, but in general the phase space of the possibilities to be tried is too large for random searches to make any progress. Instead, the learner has to construct a mental model of the situation. We can think of deep learning as adding constraints to the model, which increasingly limit the phase space. This is in accord with our common experience, that if we understand how a device works we will try a more limited combination of switches to achieve a desired outcome. The environment here provides feedback to the learner which further narrows the search, where the environment may or may not include a teacher.

Given that the motivation for learning requires a goal, then the motivation for constructivist learning amongst peers requires a common goal. Thus, an authentic context for constructivist methodology is the collaborative solution of a problem. Clearly, the teacher has to be part of that collaboration, however self-directed the pedagogy, but an important feature will be student collaboration, or in other words, some sort of group or teamwork.

The outcome of this discussion of learning is that we have set the foundations for some sort of constructivist or constructionist project-based, or problem-based, or enquiry approach, pursued through collaborative group work. We look next at the origins of problem-based learning in higher education and the problem-based edu-ecosystems that have sprung up around it.

2.4 History of problem-based approaches

Having established the educational rationale for a problem-led approach in higher education, we look here at some of the history of the idea [15]. The term PBL appears to have been coined by Woods [16] in the chemistry department at McMaster University in Canada, but the holistic implementation of PBL in university teaching is generally attributed to the medical school at that institution. This was motivated by a contradiction, that is more apparent in the training of GPs than in more academic contexts, between developing the ability of students to answer examination questions on material learnt in the lecture room and the ability to respond to patients in professional practice [17]. The success of the approach led to the adoption of PBL by medical schools in the Dutch city of Maastricht and in the Australian city of Newcastle. In all of these cases, the curriculum was newly created for the institution. By the 1990s, PBL had spread to other professional disciplines including law, psychology, education, economics and architecture. (See the references in [15].) In this diffusion, the characteristics of the pedagogy underwent adaptation to local contexts and modifications to encompass other forms of problem or project led approaches, as mentioned in section 1.7. Let us look at these variations.

PBL in medicine has these characteristics:
- a hook that excites students' interest in the problem. This is the patient presenting symptoms. More generally this can be a newspaper article (real or invented), a letter, a research report, a picture or pictures, for example, as a comic strip, and so on.
- a trigger that incites action. This is the requirement to diagnose the symptoms. In this medical context, the link with the hook is obvious and Azer [18] combines the hook and trigger in describing PBL in medicine. In a different context, for example, an AI screening programme, the trigger might be to classify the symptoms rather than to account for them.
- a scenario: the context in which the problem is to be addressed. Again in the medical model this is obvious, but in general students will be guided to what sort of response is required as defined by the context; for example, a presentation, report, research paper, podcast and so on.

The problem is then addressed by a group of students with a facilitator in attendance. The facilitator guides the students to think about the existing knowledge they might bring to bear on the problem and to list the further investigations they need to carry out, either in researching textbook knowledge or on the patient. The students will then individually consult the textbooks (or attend lectures), possibly meet as a group without a facilitator present, and reassemble to evaluate progress through a number of iterations.

It is not an accident that PBL arose in medicine, where subject knowledge has a short half-life and professional skills are key. The professional context provides a ready supply of graded problems for students to work through. The real-life context has been manipulated to provide a structured educational framework. The problems are messy and ill-structured, but in a controlled way. PBL problems are often described as 'open-ended', but while it is true that the problems may be complex and there be more than one path to a correct diagnosis, there is in fact only one correct diagnosis in each case. (There may be different opinions on the appropriate treatment.)

In disciplines other than medicine the professional context will be different. An engineer may be called upon to diagnose a fault, but her tasks are likely to be more project-oriented. Conversely, engineering projects may well be open-ended, in the sense of admitting multiple appropriate outcomes, some of which may circumvent the learning objectives (nicely encapsulated by Rita's response in Education Rita to the problem of staging Ibsen's Peer Gynt, to 'do it on the radio'.) The support from the instructor in these cases could be rather different from that in the medical model.

In consequence, PBL has been adapted in various ways even within the medical field. (The McMaster program was directed specifically at the training of general practitioners.) Along with the adaptations have come a number of other descriptions. For example, the University of Aalborg has adopted PO-PBL—project-oriented problem-based learning. The literature contains much discussion of what exactly is the difference between project- and problem-based learning. The discussion is I think confused by the absence of a distinction between the two types of project commonly employed in higher education. The one with which most physicists are familiar is the capstone research project. If this is done as a genuine research project—that is with an outcome that is not already known to the supervisor—then it is, to my mind, archetypal PBL, lacking only the group element. (Although, rather than lacking anything, it benefits from the 1–1 interaction with the supervisor as a facilitator.) Unlike that for a doctorate, the assessment is of the execution rather than the novelty of the research outcome per se. The other use of the term 'project' is the execution of a set task assessed through the extent to which the outcome meets the pre-established criteria (although there may be some assessment of process as well). The project generates a new artefact rather than specifically new knowledge. Writing a computer program for a specified task would be an obvious example. This is distinct from PBL, but can nevertheless satisfy the requirements for learning that we set out above.

In the field of law, the problem might be not to prosecute or defend a case but to diagnose a known outcome. If the case is presented as a hook to learning (rather than as an exercise on material previously delivered), this would be described as case-based learning. Business and management are areas that are replete with case analyses as approaches.to learning. One might say that cases present problems for the student (for analysis) rather than to the student (to solve). In circumstances where this provides sufficient motivation and intrinsic feedback to achieve the learning objectives, the distinction between case-based and problem-based is to my mind moot. In contrast, analysing how another GP made a diagnosis seems to be very different from the task of doing it oneself.

If cases are to promote learning, then they must involve new knowledge and hence research on the part of the student. Why then, one might argue, not skip the dressing up of learning objectives in complex cases and go straight to the research. Research-based learning proposes essentially just this. (Not to be confused with another use of the term in which students are engaged in collaborative research with academic researchers [19, 20]). Students are given a topic, and a guide to the resources required to research the topic. Having read up the material and attempted some exercises or discussion points, students come together in a workshop or seminar, which can provide feedback on their research. When we implemented this in the 1990s for all of the core material in Physics the only resources available were print materials and audio tapes. The research consisted of reading the relevant section of the textbook (or listening to an audio tape as well) and doing the end-of-chapter exercises with the help of problem-solving lectures (which did not repeat the textbook material) class workshops (in groups) and group tutorials. With the development of electronic media, the research can consist of listening to, or watching lecture snippets, and with software linked to mobile phones or keypads ('clickers') the classes can involve audience surveys. This version of research-based learning has come to be known as 'flipped learning'. The 'flip' refers to the fact that the students are presented with exercises and reading material before coming to the related class rather than as (or rather as well as) homework after the class [21].

The simplest form of a problem-based approach is enquiry: the problem is to find out something and, better still, do something with that knowledge. The outcome is not knowledge that is new to the world, but new to the student, and possibly presented or used in a novel way. Any particular implementation of learning by enquiry is characterised by the extent to which instructors relinquish control to the students, and by the nature of the enquiry.

At one extreme, the ceding of control can amount to no more than asking students to read certain articles on a topic and to write an essay on the topic, including some specified points. In physics, the Washington school have designed step-by-step tasks that challenge the learner to interact with a practical set-up in order to gain conceptual understanding [22]. At least such tightly scripted learning activities address the issue of working in the zone of proximal development. They do this by providing frequent, indeed almost continuous, feedback which students can then act on. But, while the provision of continual intrinsic feedback satisfies one of our criteria, I remain to be convinced that it allows students to see the overall goal from working through the procedures, as we discussed above.

At the other extreme, students would determine the syllabus and the nature of the assessment, either individually or as a group. I do not know any examples of this extreme. Even when students are partners in the course design there is usually a framework of learning objectives, although these do not have to be content-driven. For example, in the History of Science, students could be allowed (encouraged?), to define their own content objectives, and could be involved in a discussion about what in general they might want from the course. (I have done this with a small tutorial size class, with rather modest objectives for historiography; it would be interesting to determine if it is feasible with a large class.)

Purists have gone a long way in this direction and invented the term PPBL—pure PBL for the framework where students are fully responsible for finding resources [23]. This allows students greater (or even complete) autonomy over the learning issues. One example we use is the Nefertiti problem (see chapter 4) which can be treated as a problem in physics (dating methods), archaeology, ethics (return of an artefact to the country of origin) and other variations. We see here perhaps why we would not want to use PPBL in a physics (or other STEM) programme. In fact, we see why we might need to adapt PBL to a context in which professional practice does not provide a supply of accessible, graded problems that can direct students to appropriate learning objectives.

None of these approaches can be guaranteed to solve motivational issues. Strategic learners may look to the summative assessment to determine their level of engagement (and other aspects of the learning environment as well—we shall come to those also). So, to enquiry, we add collaboration.

2.5 Enquiry and collaboration

From what we have said about the historical development, we can characterise the different problem-based approaches in terms of enquiry and collaboration.

Note first that collaboration and enquiry are independent aspects of pedagogy in that one can have either without the other. But, enquiry learning becomes higher impact if it is linked to collaboration for two reasons: motivation and feedback. We shall look at each in turn.

We shall see that a sense of community is one key to motivating student engagement. Working together formally can promote a sense of community (with some caveats we shall get to). Team-based learning [24] can be used to motivate associative learning. There are various ways of doing this, but the main idea is to show how teams can answer questions better than individuals, something that will come as no surprise to pub quizzers. The team does this by pooling their knowledge, a process of communication that requires members of the team to articulate, and therefore formulate, their understanding and to engage in argument. This offers opportunities for multiple representations of knowledge: reading, speaking, listening and revising. While this is motivational, it does not necessarily lead to learning: students can tend to remember their own false arguments, rather than the correct outcome of discussion—as anyone who has watched a tv quiz show and tried to recall the questions and answers afterwards will testify.

Adding enquiry to collaborative learning provides a framework or scaffolding into which new information can be accommodated. Anyone who has conducted interviews with students will know that they are generally most articulate when talking about their project work, which will have been executed in a group of at least the student and the supervisor. These interactions often naturally adapt to learning styles (reading text, drawing a diagram, listening). The learning cycles we discussed above all involve interaction either with a teacher or with peers. That interaction is strongly motivated when there is a task to execute that can provide intrinsic feedback, so that the student themselves can start to form a judgement on progress. End-of-chapter exercises can fill this role for sufficiently motivated students, who will often form impromptu homework groups. Formalising this activity in organised group work means that all students can potentially benefit.

One of the challenges hinges on the distinction between a group and a team. A homework team that distributes the supposedly individual assessment by assigning questions to members, who simply then share their work, is an efficient mark-harvesting team, but not a functioning learning group. Plagiarism checks are usually enough to suppress, if not to eliminate this. Students who discuss their work together, while writing up individual submissions, form an effective group.

2.6 Research–teaching nexus

The variety of problem-based approaches has arisen through the differing demands of different disciplines and the way in which they exhibit the links between teaching and research. Let us then recap the general features of problem-based approaches [25]:

- A curriculum organised round problems, not disciplines or sub-disciplines and with emphasis on cognitive skills
- Facilitated active learning in small groups
- Learning motivated by a problem-based approach and development of life skills

We have seen that PBL in the professions is based around problems that professionals actually encounter. We have argued that this presents difficulties in subjects like physics, where the research questions make no sense to the beginning students. Diagnosing a simple case is authentic for medicine, as is a simple design task for an engineer or an architect. Authentic theoretical problems in research physics are not only unsolvable for undergraduates, but not even comprehensible. It is not simply a question of looking up the meaning of words: the explanations would make no sense without a considerable grounding. This leads to artificial problems such as 'consider a massless elephant' or a 'spherical cow' (and sometimes, nonsense ones as we remarked above [3]), which are highly demotivating. (Any amusement wears thin very rapidly.) Claims that undergraduate programmes are research-led in any significant way are not supported by the evidence [26, 27]. In their review of the literature of the extent to which a good teacher was also an effective researcher, Hattie and Marsh state that the common belief that teaching and research were inextricably intertwined is an enduring myth. At best, teaching and research are very loosely coupled [28].

In theory, practical problems provide a context for theory. But, trying to teach new physics theory in an exercise on experimental design leads to cognitive overload. At best, we can use the practical problem as a motivation. See section 5.2.

Instead of looking at content, we have to look at what it is that professional physicists do, namely the *process* of research. We shall find that research has many aspects that make research a developmental activity. The scaffolding of a problem-based approach takes the student through these levels. These levels of the research–teaching nexus have been widely discussed [28, 29]. The discussion dates back to Boyer's distinction between the different meanings of what he referred to as scholarship. These are summarised in table 2.1 [30].

The first three of Boyer's scholarships can also be thought of as the stages of development of a researcher. Figure 2.2, based on various versions in the literature [28, 31, 32], presents a version of the research–teaching nexus that develops this idea [33].

Let us look at each of the quadrants in this figure, starting with the student as receiver. Research briefed activity brings research content into the curriculum. It can be motivational in the core curriculum, but is usually only significant in higher years. Even there, supposedly research topics often present basic material that is current only in name: relativity theory is a hundred years old, the theory of the laser and superconductivity at least 50 years. On the other hand graphene (and related two-dimensional materials), quantum computing and exoplanets are examples of genuinely frontier topics that are now making an appearance in many physics curricula.

Table 2.1. Boyer's varieties of scholarship [30]. © 2014. Advance HE. All rights reserved.

Scholarship of discovery	Engage in inquiry-based learning; undergraduate research and consultancy projects; co-research projects with staff
Scholarship of integration	Engage in integrating material from different sources, including across disciplines; integrate life and work experience with academic studies; reflect on implications of studies for personal development
Scholarship of application/ engagement	Engage with local, national and international community service projects; volunteering; knowledge exchange projects; apply knowledge and skills in work-based placements
Scholarship of teaching and learning	Engage in mentoring; peer support and assessment; collaborative group work; learners as explicit partners in educational development and inquiry

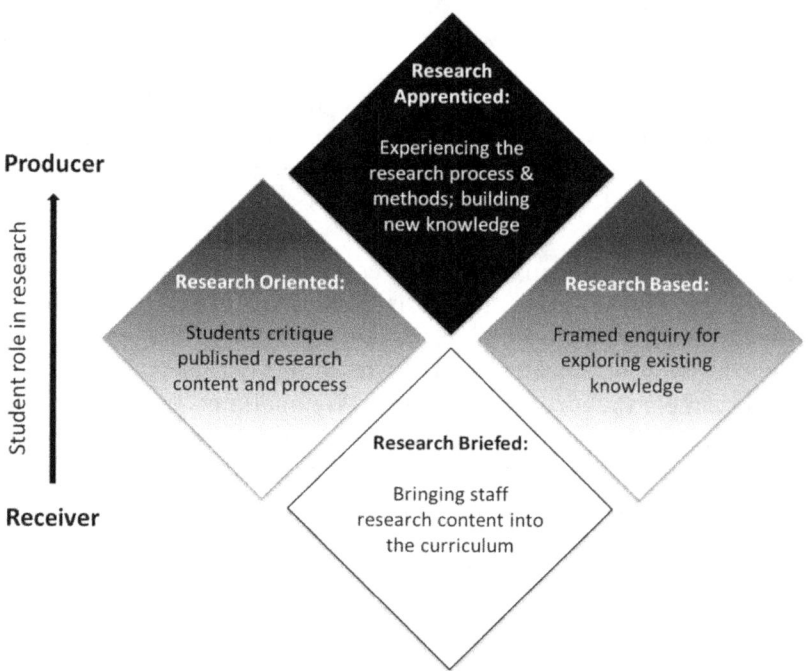

Figure 2.2. The research–teaching nexus.

Research-oriented activity, in which students undertake literature reviews, are viable where the literature is accessible, which varies considerably between disciplines. A critique of published research does not mean that students are expected to find the flaws in it!—merely to present it in some way, for example, modelled on literature reviews in research group meetings. Historic papers are often accessible, although not normally what is meant by bringing research into the curriculum.

Research apprenticed is the term used here to indicate a research activity that builds new knowledge, undertaken in conjunction with an experienced researcher as a supervisor.

This leaves us with research-based: students experience the research process. Thus, they adopt the stance of professional physicists not professional students. Traditionally, this is introduced as part of the apprenticeship of the final-year project, when students are deemed to be ready for independent advanced work. In fact, in such a structure, students coming to their project are often unprepared for the experience. The capacity for an undergraduate to undertake research has to be developed. That process needs to start early, so that students are prepared to gain the most benefit from immensively resource-intensive capstone projects. Such preparation is provided in a problem-based approach from the outset, through a thorough grounding in the various aspects of the research process.

Ideally, the delivery of a problem-based approach would include one-to-one tutorials, or small group tutorials, where the group is small enough to facilitate one-to-one interactions. (For example, capstone projects are often carried out with pairs of students.) This brings us back to the fundamental problem of mass education: how to provide the experience of individual tuition without individual tutors. So far, we have discussed collaboration and group working. In the context of the research–teaching nexus, note that these are not arbitrary add-ons, but are also authentic features of the professional research environment. Information technology is also part of the research infrastructure, so it too can make an authentic contribution, for example, in the provision of resources, feedback and collaborative tools.

2.7 Technology

Let us start with the uncontroversial fact that IT makes the provision of resources easier. Writing lecture notes may have become more time consuming, because they demand higher production values than handwritten pages, but, now that computers and smartphones are ubiquitous, the marginal cost of distributing text is essentially zero. Over time such resources build up. Our Natural Sciences programme will have had something over 2000 pages of full-colour handouts. Library resources are in principle also more readily available.

Ready availability is not the same as instant gratification. So, students have to learn that the answer to their query may not be available in a half-page, or that what they have found may be quite wrong. Instructors also need to check questions for answers on the web, if the questions are supposed to test students' understanding rather than their information retrieval skills.

We are not restricted to text to support problem-based approaches. Video lectures are widespread, but mostly only as supplementary recordings of live events, and are often of low quality. The increased use of video seems to require a culture shift. We seem to have no difficulty in reading books written by academics from outside the home institution, but apparently watching an academic from a different university deliver a pre-recorded lecture is not considered value for money. In any case, the lecture format is wholly archaic. If the natural attention span were an hour, there might be some logic in delivering material in one hour chunks. But, it is not. Material would best be delivered in shorter units. Recording makes this viable. In discussing the research on flipped learning, Bormann [34] quoting [35] reports that teachers felt it was important that the videos could be viewed in (less than) 20 minutes. A majority of students also wanted videos to last less than 20 minutes and preferred edited videos that were more concise and had higher production values [36]. Even with these overheads pre-recorded material frees up staff time in the long run for more interactive teaching.

An evident application of technology is in the use of collaborative tools. Electronic submission and marking is an obvious example, as is students working collaboratively on assignments. The use of IT also means we can deploy tests automatically. These can be MCQs and variants, but there is also progress with free text answers [37]. Many staff have also experimented with the use of audio recordings for giving feedback, with claims that this is not only more efficient but also more effective.

In theory, simulations should enable students to explore the world behind the appearance. Virtual reality could allow us to travel close to light speed, or to get down amongst the wave function. In practice, the development of the pedagogy of simulations is still in its infancy. Too often students are presented with a screen which they cannot interpret, or where it is not clear what activating the controls actually does in terms of the world outside the simulation. So, students end up exploring the workings of the code rather than the simulated world—discovering the effect of moving a slider marked temperature does not feel the same as heating a mixture. In other cases, the micro-world is represented unrealistically: for example, electrons (dots on the screen) flow unimpeded along a wire (1d tube). Some attempts have been made to design simulations by studying the way in which students respond [38]. In any case, the resources required to implement virtual worlds are beyond the scope of the education sector and will be delivered only when we have relativistic and quantum games from the deeper pockets of the video games industry.

A different solution is provided by what are called on-screen experiments pioneered by groups at Hamburg and at the Open University [39]. In these, multiple stop-motion photographs are taken of possible trajectories through a laboratory experiment, including possible errors (not switching on the power supply). The student is then presented with a 'real' experiment on the screen, which can provide intrinsic feedback. The use of remotely controlled laboratory experiments is another potential development that avoids duplication of expensive equipment whilst providing state-of-the-art practical experience.

2.8 Constructive alignment: design science

We have now discussed the ingredients for successful learning. The key to implementation is the constructive alignment of all of these aspects: structures, tools and intended outcomes. My argument is that alignment can be fully achieved only at the programme level.

The case for putting alignment at the centre of curriculum design has been argued most forcibly by Biggs [12]. Simplistically, constructive alignment means aligning the learning activities with the learning outcomes. One might think this obvious, but I have sat in many an undergraduate lecture in the process of peer review of teaching, where I could see no connection with the stream of information and what the students were meant to do with it, and, more importantly, on interrogation, nor could the lecturer provide one. ('I just think they should see this stuff'.) On the other hand, alignment has been criticised for not being clear about what it is that is aligned. Biggs says 'the verbs' [12]; that is, what the student is supposed to do is aligned with what the learning activity does. The specific criticism of this is that it is not operationalised: it does not tell the teacher what to do to create such alignment. So, a learning objective, understand the second law, does not help the teacher design an activity in which the students go about understanding the second law [40]. I think this criticism misses the point as far as application to the design of the curriculum is concerned. Alignment impacts motivation and assessment as well as delivery. So, at the level of curriculum design, there is indeed much to be aligned, which, although now increasingly evident, was totally absent in my experience at the start of my career in teaching.

Students enter university with certain existing knowledge and expectations. Their existing knowledge is almost always patchy. In physics, they generally lack much experience of extended (multi-step) problem-solving, which has not been broken down for them into single steps. They have been shielded from advanced mathematics applied to physics, whereas this will form much of the content of an undergraduate programme. Concomitantly, they believe that the exciting bits of physics involve waffle about expanding universes and lasers and that Ohm's law and the principle of the lever are boring. Their aim is to get a degree on the understanding that this will open doors to a vast variety of different employments.

Academic staff, on the other hand, have been selected for their ability to apply mathematics to physics with enjoyment. The exciting bits of physics for them are their research interests, and they are usually not involved in teaching areas in which their expertise is patchy. (Or if they are, then they can easily mug it up so that it is not patchy.) They therefore find it difficult to understand what the problems might be for students. Their objective is to recruit research students (if not for themselves alone, then for the community). Only on the matter of Ohm's law and levers, are they probably aligned with the students.

We need to move away from such misalignment. To start with, a key principle of alignment is to build on pre-existing knowledge. Ausbel says that this is the one thing you need to do if you do nothing else:

The most important single factor influencing learning is what the learner already knows. Ascertain this and teach him accordingly [41].

The traditional pedagogy in higher education almost certainly fails at this. Finding the lowest common denominator of the syllabi that beginning students will have studied is useful as a starting point, but far from a complete answer. The problem is that whatever the syllabus says, students come with incomplete knowledge and multiple misconceptions. One approach therefore is to have 'remedial classes' for first-year students. Labelling students in this way is immediately disincentivising, such that in many instances I have seen, many of those students for whom the classes are intended absent themselves. We shall see how problem-based tuition, by allowing for flexibility in prior knowledge, enables us to address this issue. There are other ways of securing alignment for the skills-based aspects of teaching, which we shall look at under personalised learning (section 2.9). The important point is that alignment here operates at the level of the curriculum as a whole.

By programme alignment, I imply more than the sequencing of content. We ought to be able to take it for granted that differential equations and vectors will be studied before they are needed in Newtonian mechanics and so on. Nevertheless, one advantage of alignment of content at the programme level is that topics can be revisited in a considered fashion.

To overcome discrepancies in alignment, students develop strategic skills to maximise the outcomes for the minimum effort. Failures in alignment, in all its aspects, thereby provide an environment in which students become professionals at what they perceive to be the objective: focussing exclusively on passing examinations.

At the course level, constructive alignment involves learning outcomes, learning activities that connect the learning outcomes to the assessments, and assessments that assess the intended learning outcomes. The problem with the focus on course-level alignment is that it becomes entirely content driven; or that it acquires some random elements of bolt-on skills, usually the group presentation. ('It was individual presentations previously, but they took too long to assess, so we changed it to groups'.)

The other failure of programme alignment occurs when an instructor decides to do something different in their course. Students fed up to this point on a diet of lectures and half-hour problems are suddenly expected to, say, research a topic for themselves and deliver a class and whatever. If this is a skills-based exercise with little new content, and appropriately supported, then it might work well. But, there has to be a rationale within the programme as to why this course is different. I have seen too many potentially good approaches fail for the lack of coherence at the programme level. I have also seen such initiatives succeed as part of a programme with clearly aligned objectives.

The problem environment created by the instructor must be accessible to the students, but in problem-based approaches, their learning needs can be met in different ways. This is achieved through the way in which the problem is scaffolded, that is, through the guidance provided by the instructor. In PBL, the learning issues at each stage are identified by the student group, perhaps with the help of the facilitator. (We shall spell this out in more detail later.) In other general versions of problem-based approaches, the instructor provides more of the framework in which the problem can be addressed, so the process is more teacher directed. We refer to this support in all cases as the scaffolding—again, more details later. The key point is that the role of the teacher changes from transmitting knowledge (from her brain or lecture notes) to that of guiding students to sources of knowledge.

However well this scaffolding is aligned, it can be short-circuited by the assessment. If the assessment turns out to require only surface learning, then this is what students (quite rationally) will do. This will damage trust for the instructor, who would be deemed to be misleading students by (in their eyes) diverting their attention from the assessment tasks. That is not to say that there is not an important place for declarative knowledge—it is impossible to think about a problem without a sound knowledge of the subject matter. A sound knowledge will include simply being able to reproduce, for example, standard proofs or dates or accounts of key historical figures or literary movements and so on. But, assessments need to go beyond this to explore what it is we are actually trying to teach (if that is indeed more than rote learning). We shall discuss meaningful assessment in the next chapter.

Our final requirement is to align a place for reflection on how and what has been learnt—metacognition and its counterpart, resilience. Developing metacognition ought to be easy. It amounts to asking: 'what would you do differently next time?' and then providing the opportunity to do it. The famous astrophysicist Subrahmanyan Chandrasekhar was said to write his scientific papers straight out in their final version. Most of us cannot do that. We respond to criticism by reworking the same academic paper with a view to improving it. But, the only times I have heard students asked the question 'what would you do differently?' is in final year vivas, where there are no opportunities to revise and resubmit. Students presumably develop a metacognitive capacity to some extent, since their final year work is usually an improvement on their year one work. In the constructionist context, the group interaction during the reworking of the artefact that they are working on to solve the set problem should develop metacognition, although it would be of interest to research how much it actually does.

In terms of lifestyle, resilience is an increasing problem for students, which may or may not have something to do with the impact of social media. That is not my concern here. What is of close relevance to problem-based approaches is resilience on the smaller scale of what to do when you are stuck (and cannot google the answer). There are for me two responses which need to be encouraged. The first is to freely associate to see if there are other ways of tackling a problem. Free association episodes at the start of a facilitation session are a common feature of problem-based approaches. In one-to-one interactions, one can take students back to what they know to discover the barriers to progress, but that is not so easy in group sessions, especially with limited time. The other approach is to get students to try to formulate the issue that is blocking progress as a question for the group or for the instructor (which of course assumes that the pedagogy encourages such questions). In this way, students begin to reflect on possible routes to progress (resilience) not on the answer (dependency).

We have discussed how students learn and how to operationalise that knowledge in curriculum design through problem-based approaches. We shall go on to spell out more of the details in the following chapters. Finally, here I want to note the research which shows that how students learn and how they think they learn can be quite different.

Students generally think they learn best through binging on revision—putting the hours in through a few long sessions rather than multiple shorter ones [42]. In fact, all the evidence shows that binging is less effective than a steady pace. The theoretical underpinning for this is the forgetting curve [43, 44]. To anticipate, we shall find that many students express a preference for a lecture-based curriculum above a problem-based approach. We shall see (chapter 6) that here too they are wrong (at least in as far as better learning is concerned).

2.9 Personalised curriculum

I began by stating the tension between one-to-one tuition and a system of mass education. We have seen how constructive alignment of problem-based approaches can be used to minimise this conflict. So far, however, we have discussed constructive alignment of the curriculum as a whole. Here I want to explore how much further we can go in aligning the educational experience for the individual student.

Given that students come with different prior knowledge and expectations, with different goals and ambitions, it would be surprising if alignment meant the same thing for every student. Thus, curricula need to provide multiple perspectives and multiple pathways [45]. Traditional curriculum design has focussed on multiple pathways, to the exclusion of multiple perspectives, by providing option modules each with largely identical structures and assessments. This uniformity is imposed in the name of equivalence. It provides limited choice, focussing only on content, which is largely arbitrary in later years of a programme (by definition, since the content is optional), while being resource intensive. If there are to be optional modules, there are ways of ensuring fairness other than by constraining the structure and assessment. For large groups, the simplest equalisation is to scale marks so that the average on each option module is equal to the average for those students on their common core modules.

Another constraint which seems illogical is the restriction in most UK institutions on the number of modules (courses) that can be taken for credit. Given the large resource that goes into providing a module the marginal cost of an extra student is small. The argument that students who have paid for 120 credits (60 ECTS) should be allowed to consume only 120 credits seems out of line with the concept of education as a public good. The range of student abilities, even in highly selective universities, can be large, in which case the notion of the workload of an average student (the metric for credits) becomes meaningless. Algorithms can be used to incorporate additional credits into degree classifications. Some institutions in the UK have allowed this at various times.

My preference for a personalised curriculum is for options within modules that allow students to explore different aspects in different ways. This is a natural extension of the problem-based approach. It allows students equipped with the basic knowledge to pursue their own research agenda. Making such further exploration optional is another way of extending the most talented students without disadvantaging the less able. Some care is needed with the assessment algorithm to include the additional work within the module envelope; we want to avoid extremes where a string of 40% marks ends up as an 'average' of 60% (say). However, it is not difficult to devise non-linear scales with thresholds. I will return to personalised curricula in section 7.5.

References

[1] Pindar 1997 *The Odes and Selected Fragments, Pythian 2, line 72* (London: Everyman Library) (More usually attributed to F Nietzsche in *Thus, Spoke Zarathustra* and the lesser known *The Gay Science*)

[2] Good T L and Brophy J E 1994 *Contemporary Educational Psychology* 5th edn (Cambridge: Pearson)

[3] Slisko J 2008 How can formulation of physics problems and exercises aid students in thinking about their results? *Latin-Am. J. Phys. Educ.* **2** 137–42

[4] Dewey J 2012 *Democracy and Education* (Start Publishing) (An e-book version of the 1916 original published by New York: Macmillan)

[5] Piaget J 1962 *Play, Dreams, and Imitation in Childhood* (New York: Norton & Co.) (see https://www.simplypsychology.org/piaget.html for a quick guide)

[6] Vygotsky L S 1978 *Mind in Society: The Development of Higher Psychological Processes* (Cambridge, MA: Harvard University Press)

[7] Bruner J 1960 *The Process of Education* (Cambridge, MA: Harvard University Press)

[8] Dewey J 1938 *Experience and Education* (New York: Kappa Delta Pi)

[9] Hattie H and Yates G 2014 *Visible Learning and the Science of How We Learn* (London: Routledge)

[10] Papert S and Harel I 1991 Situating constructionism *Constructionism: Research Reports and Essays, 1885–1900* ed I Harel and S Papert (Norwood, NJ: Ablex Publishing Company)

[11] Bloom B S, Engelhart M D, Furst E J, Hill W H and Krathwohl D R 1956 *Taxonomy of Educational Objectives: The Classification of Educational Goals. Handbook I: Cognitive Domain* (New York: David McKay) (Bloom's editorship of this work led to the appelation. There are literally hundreds of guides on the web)

[12] Biggs J and Tang C 2011 *Teaching for Quality Learning at University* (New York: SRHE & Open University Press)

[13] Kolb D A 1984 *Experiential Learning: Experience as the Source of Learning and Development* (Englewood Cliffs, NJ: Prentice Hall)

[14] Ambrose S, Bridges M, DiPietro M, Lovett M and Norman M 2010 *How Learning Works; 7 Research-Based Principles for Smart Teaching* (San Francisco, CA: Jossey-Bass)

[15] de Graaff E and Kolmos A 2007 History of problem-based and project-based learning *Management of Change: Implementation of Problem-based and Project-based Learning in Engineeering* ed E E de Graaff and A Kolmos (Sense Publishers) (available at http://inelmen.boun.edu.tr/emi/publ08/sefi08/eric07sefi.pdf)

[16] Woods D R 1994 *Problem-Based Learning: How to Gain the Most from PBL* (Waterdown, ON: Donald R Woods)

[17] Spaulding W P 1969 The undergraduate medical curriculum model: McMaster University *Can. Med. Assoc. J.* **100** 659–64

[18] Azer S 2008 *Navigating Problem-Based Learning* (Marrickville: Churchill Livingstone)

[19] Lambert C 2009 Pedagogies of participation in higher education: a case for research-based learning *Pedagogy Culture Soc.* **17** 295–309

[20] Healey M, Flint A and Harrington K 2014 Engagement through partnership: students as partners in learning and teaching in higher education (https://www.heacademy.ac.uk/system/files/resources/engagement_through_partnership.pdf)

[21] O'Flaherty J and Phillips C 2015 The use of flipped classrooms in higher education: A scoping review *Internet Higher Educ.* **25** 85–95

[22] McDermott L 1996 *Physics by Inquiry* (New York: Wiley)

[23] Phillips D C 2014 *Encyclopedia of Educational Theory and Philosophy* (New Delhi: Sage Publications) p 655

[24] Michaelsen L K and Sweet M 2008 The essential elements of team-based learning *New Direct. Teach. Learn.* **116** https://doi.org/10.1002/tl.330

[25] Walton H J and Mathews M B 1989 Essentials of problem-based learning *Med. Educ.* **23** 542–58

[26] Gibbs G 2010 *Dimensions of Quality* (York: Higher Education Academy) (https://www.heacademy.ac.uk/system/files/dimensions_of_quality.pdf)

[27] Hattie J and Marsh H W 1996 The relationship between research and teaching: a metaanalysis *Rev. Educ. Res.* **66** 507–42

[28] Healey M 2005 Linking research and teaching to benefit student learning *J. Geogr. Higher Educ.* **29** 183–201

[29] Griffiths R 2004 Knowledge production and the research–teaching nexus: the case of the built environment disciplines *Stud. Higher Educ.* **29** 709–26

[30] Boyer 1998 Commission on Educating Undergraduates in the Research University Reinventing undergraduate education: a blueprint for Americaas research universities (available at https://files.eric.ed.gov/fulltext/ED424840.pdf)

[31] Levy P and Petrulis R 2012 How do first-year university students experience inquiry and research, and what are the implications for the practice of inquiry-based learning? *Stud. Higher Educ.* **37** 85–101

[32] Walkington H 2015 *Students as researchers: supporting undergraduate research in the disciplines in higher education* (York: Higher Education Academy) (https://www.heacademy.ac.uk/system/files/resources/Students%20as%20researchers_1.pdf)

[33] Gretton S N, Harvey C T, Lock P E, Williams D P, Hurkett C P, Symons S L and Raine D J Revisiting the research: teaching nexus framework: two case studies introducing research into programme level, undergraduate teaching (unpublished)

[34] Bormann J 2014 Affordances of flipped learning and its effects on student engagement and achievement *Graduate Research Papers* **137** https://scholarworks.uni.edu/grp/137

[35] Mason G, Shuman T and Cook K 2013 Comparing the effectiveness of an inverted classroom to a traditional classroom in an upper-division engineering course *IEEE Trans. Educ.* **56** 430–35

[36] Enfield J 2013 Looking at the impact of the flipped classroom model of instruction on undergraduate multimedia students at CSUN *Techtrends* **57** 14–27

[37] Jordan S 2012 Student engagement with assessment and feedback: some lessons from short-answer free-text e-assessment questions *Comput. Educ.* **58** 818–34

[38] Kohnle A *et al* 2013 A new introductory quantum mechanics curriculum *Eur. J. Phys.* **35** 015001

[39] Hatherly P A, Jordan S E and Cayless A 2009 Interactive screen experiments—innovative virtual laboratories for distance learners *Eur. J. Phys.* **30** 751

[40] Laurillard D 2012 *Teaching as a Design Science: Building Pedagogical Patterns for Learning and Technology* (New York: Routledge)
[41] Ausubel D P 1968 *Educational Psychology: A Cognitive View* (New York: Holt, Rinehart and Winston)
[42] Kornell N and Bjork R A 2007 The promise and perils of self—regulated study *Psychonom. Bull. Rev.* **14** 219–24
[43] Ebbinghaus H 1913 Memory: A contribution to experimental psychology (http://psychclassics.yorku.ca/Ebbinghaus/index.htm) translated from the 1885 German edition by Henry Ruger & Clara Bussenius (Teachers College NY)
[44] Murre J M J and Dros J 2015 Replication and analysis of Ebbinghaus' forgetting curve *PLoS ONE* **10** e0120644
[45] Walkington C and Bernacki M L 2014 Motivating students by 'personalizing' learning around individual interests: a consideration of theory, design, and implementation issues *Motiv. Interv.* **18** 139–76

IOP Publishing

Problem-Based Approaches to Physics
Changing perspectives in higher education
Derek Jeffrey Raine

Chapter 3

Alignment

3.1 Outcomes

We ended the previous chapter with a discussion of alignment. The starting point for alignment is the programme outcomes: what it is that we want our graduates to obtain from their time at university. Outcomes are usually framed in terms of learning objectives, which represent an attempt to operationalise the aims of a degree programme as lists of measurable items. To the extent that outcomes specify what students can do, they align with our discussion of what it takes to learn something. The 'doing words' also help to specify the level at which graduates would be expected to achieve each outcome. As an example, in the previous chapter, we met the well-known Bloom's taxonomy [1], one of a multitude of structures in the literature by which we can articulate and differentiate learning outcomes. As an illustration, a modification of Bloom's hierarchy in ascending order of cognitive skill is: recall, understand, apply, analyse, evaluate, create [2].

At the base level ('define', 'state', 'recall', etc), this is straightforward: there are some things that students just need to know. As an example from physics, take the formula for kinetic energy: $K = 1/2mv^2$. This concept was originally proposed by Leibnitz as what he called *vis viva*, but without the factor of 1/2. The factor of 1/2 (and the fact that it is now called kinetic energy) is just a useful later convention, which has to be learnt, and that learning can be straightforwardly tested.

Let us take as another example the relation between distance, time and speed: $v = d/t$. The student can learn this by rote and will be able to demonstrate whether they know it. They may even apply it by substituting numbers from a word-problem. But, we want more than that. We want them to understand that the formula encapsulates what it is that we mean by the concept of speed. The relationship is not just a convention; it embodies the way in which we describe the world. Now, I do not know how to test unequivocally for this level of understanding. I can couch a learning outcome as 'explain the formula', but the diligent student can then restate the explanation I have provided. I can only offer students the opportunity to use the formula until it becomes (or in the hope that it becomes) internalised.

Ideally, we would like students to see that the formula $v = d/t$ is not just about moving bodies, but applies to all change at a uniform rate. (So, students might relate it to some aspect of their current understanding such as that an hourly rate of pay is total pay divided by the number of hours worked.) In other words, we want students to generalise or transfer knowledge.

As a further example to illustrate the problem, students of physics almost always learn the concept of 'half-life' in the context of radioactive decay. It is the time it takes for half of the radioactive atoms in a sample to disintegrate. But, they need to be aware that the concept applies to any exponential decay, not just radioactivity decay (I'd like to quip that a dead body has a half-life, although it is not quite true, since the decay of body heat after death is not strictly exponential.) So, to address this, let us say that we frame a learning objective as: apply the concept of half-life to exponential decay (Bloom's level 3). We have thereby done the generalisation for the students. The students can now carry out the assigned task, but they have not really learnt what the task was for. It seems to be a case of measurement (or measurability) destroying the system we are trying to measure. In other words, by operationalising our learning objectives as outcomes they may become too granular, and fail to convey the overall purpose of the course. Other issues with learning outcomes are widely discussed in the literature [3].

This is important, because problem-solving is a combination of learnt models transferred to novel situations. It requires both factors: the memorised (internalised) model calculations and the ability to transfer or extend them. Traditional approaches tend to undermine this in both regards. The de-emphasising of rote learning of proofs reduces the stock of models that students have to draw on, and posing the problems as end-of-chapter exercises (or in carefully structured step-wise examination questions) undermines practice at generalisation (since the requisite general concept is obviously somewhere in the chapter).

Now, the granular application of learning outcomes is further undermined by the rather obvious fact that we do not require 100% compliance. So, what does it mean to say that a student has achieved 50% of the learning outcomes? Does it mean that they can always be trusted to get things half wrong? The issue is often addressed by benchmarking—the specification of minimum and typical standards. But, this does not really get around the problem, unless we are willing to fail students who do not reach every one of the minimum specifications. (The fact that we are not is evidence that we do not really believe that graduateness can be defined by learning outcomes.) We shall see how any attempt to answer these questions requires us to examine what it is that we are assessing for (section 3.4). Here I am merely making the point that learning outcomes, as usually conceived in operationalised form, while they may have many benefits [4], are not sufficient to characterise a university education. I am not going to be concerned with whether or not problem-based approaches are better or worse at satisfying granular learning outcomes (a matter to which we shall return in chapter 6).

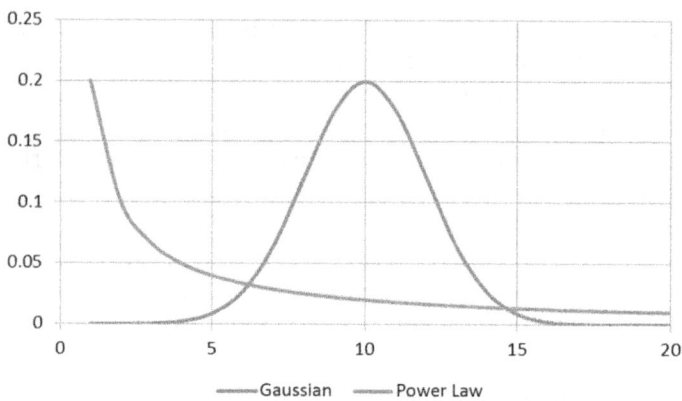

Figure 3.1. The distribution of talent (power law) compared to a Gaussian.

To see what we need to be aiming for in discussing outcomes as drivers of curriculum design, consider figure 3.1 which shows how talent is distributed across various groups of people. The graph shows a power-law distribution as observed [5] compared to the normal or Gaussian distribution as usually assumed. We can conclude that fitting Gaussian distributions to power laws has unintended consequences. These have been spelt out in the context of hiring and firing in business, but they have relevance to education too. We need to be aware that a power-law distribution means that there is no such agent as the representative (average) student. We should not be framing learning outcomes and their assessments for this mythical entity.

It is interesting to try to connect the distribution of talent with learning theory. Donner and Hardy [6] show how individual learning curves involve the crossing of thresholds. They fit a power law to the approach to the thresholds, but also show that exponential works almost as well. On this view, the extent of achievement of an individual learner will depend on the number of thresholds crossed. This will depend on the time to reach each threshold and the total time on task. Ericsson *et al* [7] show that the time on task dominates over intrinsic differences in ability in acquiring expert behaviour (i.e. observed talent), although intrinsic attributes may influence the amount of time spent practicing. To see how the power law might arise, consider that the rate of learning increases with the number of things already learnt—that is, the number of thresholds already crossed—and that this dependence is linear. Then the observed talent T will depend exponentially on the time on task t, $T = \exp(\lambda t)$. We can interpret the individual learning curves in terms of a Poisson probability distribution of the practice times to cross each threshold, $p(t_s) = p_0 \exp(-\mu t_s)$. If we now assume that the probability of time on task follows the same exponential law, $p(t) = p_0 \exp(-\mu t)$, we can eliminate t to obtain a power-law distribution of talent $\propto T^{-\mu/\lambda}$ as observed by O'Boyle and Aguinis [5]. (For those interested in a more rigorous approach, the power law can be derived from a Yule process with exponential lifetimes [8].)

Our use of thresholds here is different from, but related to that of, threshold concepts thought of as troublesome gateways to new understanding. Cousins [9] provides a very brief introduction, and some references to the original work on threshold concepts. On the one hand, thresholds refer to multiple small steps in learning, and on the other to major transitions. It is interesting to think of the two aspects as extremes of a continuum in which we view learning as avalanches of adjustments of neuronal connections. Such avalanches might themselves be expected to obey a power-law size distribution [10], the totality of which would be influenced by time on task and individual talent.

It is interesting to speculate how the fitting of Gaussian outcomes to power-law distributions might explain why small shifts in the class boundary at first class, or between pass and fail, can have large consequences in the distribution of outcomes; or, to put it the other way round, why the large change in degree class distributions in recent years in the UK is not necessarily an indicator of large changes in standards.

3.2 Engagement

Another aspect of alignment is a sense of community; so what is a sense of community?

> Sense of community is a feeling that members have of belonging, a feeling that members matter to one another and to the group, and a shared faith that members' needs will be met through their commitment to be together [11].

We shall start with why a sense of community is important and then move on to how it is achieved.

Surveys [12, 13] have been used in North America, Australasia and parts of Asia to evaluate student engagement with their courses as a proxy for educational effectiveness, rather than, as happens in the UK, to assess student satisfaction. In the UK, a number of institutions have participated in the engagement questionnaire (UKES) run by the Higher Education Academy (now part of Advance HE). Amongst other things, the UKES [14] asks questions about community. For example:

Q3. During the current academic year, about how often have you done each of the following?
    3.1.a. Worked with other students on course projects or assignments
    3.2.a. Explained course material to one or more students
    3.3.a. Asked another student to help you understand course material
    3.4.a. Prepared for exams or assessments by discussing or working through course material with other students

The results show that community and engagement (measured by time-on-task) are correlated. This is consistent with NSS results, which show also that sense of community and student satisfaction are correlated. Furthermore, our own survey of University of Leicester students shows that around 80% judge their work ethic by comparison with other students. This is true both for students who report a high workload, and for those who claim to spend relatively little time on their studies. A sense of community seems to be stronger in departments where the dispersion in workload is smaller. While we cannot demonstrate the direction of cause and effect, since we cannot directly influence the dispersion in work ethic, it is tempting to hope that the creation of a sense of community would lead to greater engagement. Research shows that students who feel they belong have a higher degree of intrinsic motivation and academic confidence [15, 16]. We shall look at how the nature of assessments can impact on both community and work ethic later.

To return then to what constitutes a sense of community, the most widely cited contribution is McMillan and Chavis [17]. They present four factors. Let us look at each in turn and relate them to higher education.

1. Membership: entry barriers define the boundaries of the community.
   - In academia, the barriers are defined by the Department (even where departments have been merged into larger entities). For students, it is sometimes the entry qualifications that define the in-group. Various prestigious institutions suffer from time to time when shared success in the competition for entry replaces a continuing work ethic in providing the sense of belonging. The student contract, or some less formal way of providing clarity as to what is expected, can be a better approach. But, a generally collaborative approach to learning might be an even better aim.
   - Membership should also create a sense of safety. In particular, universities should be safe places to experience failure, because this is how the student explores their personal potential. This is not the same as being protected from ideas that one might not like.
   - A community should provide a sense of belonging, which can come only through working together, so that students and staff are personally invested in the success of the programme.
   - Finally under membership, McMillan and Chavis mention a common symbol system. I know some programmes have their own hoodies or jerseys, but this aspect of membership is more often observed through common ritual than through common apparel. I include here the ritual of lectures, where attendance provides absolution from the actual work of teaching and learning (for both staff and students). The communal activity is important, but it needs to be more than a rite of membership.

2. Influence: We need to create an environment where members feel that they have a say in what happens. The appearance of student–staff committees is intended to address this point, but they cannot be effective where academic staff themselves do not feel they have much influence in their institution.

3. Integration and fulfillment of needs: this brings us back to constructive alignment, but now in the wider setting of both cognitive and affective domains. It is in this area where we appear to have experienced a large deterioration in provision in recent years, despite the increase in resources

and heightened awareness of the need for emotional support. The once-prized tutorial system in the UK has bent under the weight of student numbers, and support is now largely outsourced to a central facility. Added to that, the role of departmental administrative support, which used to be a first point of contact for pastoral care, and crucial to the creation of a departmental community, appears to be diminished. This might be a rewarding area for research.
4. Shared emotional connection: English is deficient in terms for distinctive forms of love, but love in the ancient Greek sense of agape, of one's discipline and its history, and the desire to share this, is characteristic of the academic research community. Communication of agape will also be a feature of a successful learning community.

So, how do we build this learning community? Let us start with the student community and student-student interactions. I believe a pedagogy of engagement can be built by multiple low-stakes group activities in, for example, workshops. These are included in many induction sessions, but then abandoned. It is important that they are low-stakes activities, where students can enjoy working together without stress. However, these need to be consistent across the programme: a sense of belonging is not (or is only weakly) generated at individual course level [15].

Gibbs cites high expectations as a crucial factor [18]. Surveys of students have suggested that they spend much less time on task during terms than module specifications would require, much less by factors of 2 or so than the 40 hours per week expected [19]. (There are claims that this is made up during holidays.) I suspect that there is almost no lower limit to the workload that many students will adopt given the opportunity. So, why the paradoxical cry for more contact hours? One explanation could be summarised in a request once made to me by a student objecting to the problem-based approach: 'tell me what you want me to know and I'll learn it'. In other words, a belief that teaching is about telling, and the more telling the better. To resolve the conflict between effective learning and student satisfaction, we need to involve students in programme design. (See section 2.9 for one of the ways in which a problem-based approach achieves this.)

Turning next to the student–staff community, I would argue that a holistic approach includes all the staff, not just the academic staff. I mentioned above the role of administrative staff who are often more accessible to students. But, they need reasonable privacy, not a busy multi-occupation open office. The teaching administrator would often have been the first to pick up mental health issues, possibly followed by a personal tutor meeting and professional intervention. The personal tutor system has broken down, not just because of tutor loading, but where there is no longer a triage stage with the firm-but-friendly teaching administrator to whom students can relate.

Finally, relationships between students and academic staff are obviously helped by an open-door policy, where staff are available during working hours. This is not practical with large staff–student ratios, nor is it reasonable that students expect staff to be available by email at all times of the day and night. On the other hand, with appropriate boundaries, electronic communication can add to a sense of community. In the best cases, the development of a learning community has become a driver for dedicated teaching staff who can devote more time to both academic and pastoral support (section 7.1).

Healey *et al* [20] have proposed a conceptual model of the staff–student partnership based around four broad areas of interest: learning, teaching and assessment; subject-based research and inquiry; scholarship of teaching and learning; curriculum design and pedagogic consultancy. The emphasis is therefore on the content of the activity—essentially what can be collaborated on. In table 3.1, we give an alternative characterisation based on where the focus of ownership lies and the depth of the collaboration.

Some of the examples in the table, such as module evaluations and the co-development of resources, are self-explanatory. Pedagogic research projects may produce learning materials and may also provide a basis for co-creation of the curriculum, as well as introducing students to the scholarship of teaching and learning. The entry under student-led research talks refers to a student initiative to invite doctoral students from across the sciences at an institution to talk to undergraduates about their work. Student conferences include an annual UK national conference for students of Natural Science programmes. The involvement of students in vacation research is increasingly widespread as an extra-curricular activity, but involves only a minority of students. The well-being initiative referred to in the table was a co-conducted event at McMaster in which students were motivated, from their own experiences with stress and mental health issues, to create a forum where they could share their experiences with younger cohorts in the same programmes.

While individual activities may involve only a minority of students, if they are not always the same minority they can involve enough of the cohort to provide a halo effect towards building a community. A problem-based approach provides a means of scaling many of the collaborations to whole-class activities.

Table 3.1. The classification framework for student–instructor partnerships according to the levels of student initiation and student involvement in partnership activities with some examples. Adapted from [21].

	Student ownership →	
Student autonomy ↓	A. Instructor initiated	B. Student initiated
Instructor led	Module evaluation	Lecture capture
		Research seminars
Co-conducted	Teaching resources	Well-being initiative
	PBL resources	
	Chemistry clips (videos)	
Student led	Research (capstone) project	Research talks
	Student conferences	Careers symposium
	Outreach projects	

3.3 Metacognition

Engagement for learning is not just a question of enthusiasm and motivation: it requires that the student reflect on their actions and profit from that reflection. Such reflection is prompted and supported by feedback. This is one of the most difficult areas of pedagogy: how to give purposive feedback with which students will engage. It is well-known that in student surveys, such as NSS, students are least happy with the feedback they receive. Let us try to unpick the issue.

I start with an example. In my experience, physics students are bad at writing mathematics correctly in formal reports. There is often no consistency in the use of a mathematics font for symbols, and no punctuation of equations; often the labelling of equations is poor, or at least, not conventional. Students do not appear to respond to my attempts to correct this. How is it that they do not copy the well-formatted mathematics in the textbooks they read? In my informal interviews with a small number of students (I have not done this systematically), two reasons emerge. On the one hand, some students do not read the mathematics at all—they skip over the equations and references to them in the text, only referring back if an exercise points them in that direction. On the other hand, some students who do read the equations read them symbol by symbol and not as sentences, rather as they started reading words by sounding out the letters. In neither case do they see that, by limiting the cognitive load, correct formatting makes a difference to the ease with which the mathematics can be read. They are in fact blind to my feedback.

This is an extreme case, but not an uninformative one. How many times have I seen feedback in the nature of 'you could provide more detail here' or 'you need to clarify this argument'. Indeed, how often, in my attempt to encourage metacognition, must I plead guilty to (uninformatively) suggesting to a student that, if they just stopped to think about a sentence they had written, they would see that it was obviously wrong!

The feedback here is all extrinsic, and for students the main carrier of information in extrinsic feedback is the mark. If the mark they get is the mark they expect, then there is no point in spending much time working on the more detailed feedback, because, so the thought goes, it will not make any difference. Before we get too smug, recall that scientists sometimes do the same thing: a paper rejected by a prestigious journal as needing more work is instead resubmitted to a less demanding publisher. On the other hand, as researchers we do at least get the opportunity to rework a paper to improve it based on referees' reports. For students, it is quite a big leap to take account of the feedback on one piece of work and used it to improve what is for them an entirely different piece.

On the other hand, where students have similar pieces of assessed work, especially where these are substantial, they do refer to feedback on previous submissions. (Again, I say this based on a small number of interviews, not on systematic research.) So, if we want to develop metacognition in circumstances where only extrinsic feedback is available, we have to provide opportunities for resubmission of work. (One of a number of suggestions in [22] based, by these authors, on research evidence.) One approach I have seen is to break larger pieces of work down, so that students learn to write a small section at a time with multiple opportunities for revision. There are various techniques of this sort in the literature with regard to teaching mathematics. The Keller plan [23, 24] or mastery learning is the most extreme, whereby students cannot proceed to the next topic until they have mastered the present one. For the mathematics courses in our Natural Sciences programme, students who do not get all the exercises correct on the first submission are required to attend a workshop where they are helped to correct their attempts. (They can get a mark for the section only if they then get 80% correct.) Rohrer [25] has shown that homework sets that include exercises that revisit old material, as well as the newly taught topic, improve student learning.

A better approach is to create a model environment that provides intrinsic feedback. In principle, laboratory experiments should provide the ideal setting, but these are more often than not constructed to work according to a script, requiring little actual engagement with the process (as opposed to the results). A realistic environment does not mean constructing experiments that do not work, even though students may learn more from diagnosing faulty equipment than from pressing the on-switch on a functioning device. A realistic laboratory environment may have more to do with sufficiently poor signal to noise that requires students to be honest about their analysis. (See chapter 5.) This type of intrinsic feedback often creates resentment, but this is largely because students expect to lose marks if they do not get the answer in the book. I think these expectations can be managed. One often sees much greater degrees of resilience when students work on research projects, where they understand that it is the process that will be assessed, not necessarily the end result. An objective of a problem-based approach is to extend this attitude to the rest of the programme.

3.4 Formative and summative assessment

Finally, we come to assessment itself.

The first requirement for feedback is that students actually do the assessment. In some environments, coming to a class unprepared is unacceptable. One can then set lots of formative assessments which, by definition, do not carry any marks. In a problem-based approach, the group meetings provide a framework for formative feedback. In other contexts, the only accepted indicator of the value of an assignment appears to be the mark it carries. Fortunately, the relationship between value and attached mark is highly non-linear. This provides the opportunity for multiple pseudo-formative assessments for small fractions of the module mark.

In order to design assessments that provide purposive feedback, we need to think about what an assessment is for. Here is a list:

1. Competency: The assessment of competency applies to well-defined tasks (the lower levels of Bloom's taxonomy) where a judgment can be made as to whether they are executed properly or not. Basic techniques in mathematics, computer programming and laboratory skills fall into this category. Students need feedback and repetition here until they get it right. Some attempt is often made to divide science examinations into a competency section and a

problem section. Unfortunately weaker students often do badly on the competency section and pass on the basis of marks randomly picked up from their attempts at the problems.

A positive feature of competency is that it is easy to assess. I have extensively used a marking system of 0, 1/2 or 1 for competency-based exercises. It is fairly easy to standardise if the marking is distributed amongst many instructors, and easy for use in peer marking and, above all, relatively quick. In peer marking, feedback becomes part of the group discussion; otherwise, it is delivered to the class based on the collated information the marking has provided for the instructor. Within workshops, it can be used in pub-quiz format. (Groups mark each other's answers.)

2. Progression: In higher education, progression is based on the end-of-year examination for admission to the next stage. It implies a minimum hurdle signifying sufficient progress to undertake a set of courses at the next higher level. The UK operates a system of higher education in which progression rates of close to 100% are expected. Sometimes progression is based partly on continuous assessment and partly on examination, with some algorithm to combine these into overall module marks. Unfortunately, the assessments are also designed to produce a rank order, so the assessments either tend to lack discrimination at the upper end (leading to grade inflation) or at the lower end (leading to pass/fail determined by noise). To compensate, an elaborate system of resit assessments are widely offered.

3. Selection: This is not the same as progression, although in both cases students proceed to a next stage. Students are selected for specific purposes according to some set of criteria. It is not expected that all applicants will be selected. In fact, criteria are often set to eliminate most of the candidates. As an example, since degree programmes are not generally designed to evaluate students' workplace potential, employers use other methods of selection. Such assessments should discriminate at the boundary i.e. produce a clear division. The traditional university programmes used to do this (more or less successfully) at the 1/2(i) class boundary for the purpose of selecting candidates for PhDs and further study.

4. Prizes: These are an extreme form of selection, with even more of a random element, especially when based on assessments designed to test other things.

5. Pass/fail: At the other extreme, rather than selecting the few best for the next stage pass/fail assessments are (or should be) designed to eliminate only the few who lack a sufficient breadth of basic competence. Such assessments should discriminate at the pass/fail boundary. The usual resit examinations, which are simply set at the level of the first examination, often fail to do this.

It is clear that not all of these objectives can be achieved in a single type of assessment and not in a single examination (or possibly in multiple examinations). Attempts to remedy this have led to the introduction of continuous assessment, where marks of 100% for competency, and fail marks for lack thereof, appear more acceptable. Continuous assessment that morphs into continual assessment does, however, lead to the problem of assessment and marking overload. In the worst cases, examination stress for the students is replaced by continuous stress about deadlines.

But, perhaps this is the wrong way of thinking about assessment; we should perhaps end with 'none of the above'. Rather, we should categorise this list as assessments *of* learning in contrast to assessments *for* learning or assessments *as* learning. Conventionally, the distinction here is between summative and formative assessment, although proponents of assessment for learning regard it as somewhat distinct from formative assessment. The distinction is between the design purpose (assessment of or for) and the function executed (formative or summative). Formative assessment per se provides students with an evaluation of their success or failure, but not necessarily on how to make further progress [26]. The important point is that 'an assessment activity can help learning if it provides information that teachers and their students can use as feedback in assessing themselves and one another and in modifying the teaching and learning activities in which they are engaged' [27, 28].

Take the student perspective first. If an activity does not provide intrinsic feedback, then as a matter of logic it has to be assessed for the student to receive any feedback at all—in other words, for it to be a learning experience. Assessment overload therefore has less to do with assessment than with the lack of time to perform the required task. Critiques of the greater learning time required in problem-based pedagogies reveal just this. Unless assignments all require qualifying passes without resubmission—that is unless students are prevented from learning from their mistakes—multiple assessments are logically largely relatively low-stakes assessments. (They cannot add to more than 100%.) A properly structured curriculum with multiple assessments (i.e. opportunities for feedback) should therefore not create a high-stress environment.

A problem-based approach can also allow students to tackle content knowledge at different levels. For example, one group might put more emphasis on the statistical analysis of data than on developing a physical model. Another group might take the problem further than the curriculum objectives, by, for example, working out a three-dimensional case instead of sticking to one dimension. One group might feel more confident discussing particular examples with less emphasis on the general theory. My point is that the problem-based approach can allow students to show through continuous assessment what they have mastered. It aligns pedagogy with the distribution of talent we discussed in chapter 2. There is some evidence that the STEM (Science, Technology, Engineering and Mathematics) gender gap is eliminated (or even reversed) in continuously assessed work [29]; in other words, that it is a better measure of talent.

From the staff perspective, giving a lot of feedback requires a lot of marking, for which they do not have time. Actually, this criticism is often mis-directed at the marking load generated by over-examination. If summative assessments do not provide useful feedback, then they should be used sparingly, only as much as is necessary to stimulate and verify student learning, specifically for basic discipline knowledge and competencies and accountability. As we have seen, formative feedback is the means by which students learn. Therefore, resources need to be organised around the delivery of formative feedback. The problem-based approach by focussing on group work is one way of directing staff time; the research-based component of this approach is another. (See [18].) The nature of the interaction with the group fulfills precisely the requirements of assessment for learning by providing opportunities for adjustments to both teaching and learning. (Of course, both have to be capable of making the adjustment: I have seen responses to student misconceptions where the instructor simply repeats a point only more slowly and more loudly, like the stereotypical Englishman abroad talking to the natives.) I will return to the question of resources in chapter 7.

3.5 Authentic assessment

We come now to what I regard as the key to curriculum design for student engagement: authentic assessment. In some way, what we attempt here is to bring some of the experience of the workplace into the safe environment of the university in what one might call learning-place working.

Let us start with what authenticity is not.

> Joe and Sal decide that little Ronny is well-behaved enough to sit at the table with the family for Thanksgiving dinner. They are wrong. Ronny throws a 150 g handful of mashed potatoes horizontally with a speed of 5 m/s. It strikes a 1.2 kg gravy boat that is initially at rest on the frictionless table. If the potatoes stick to the gravy boat, what is the speed of the combined system as it slides down the table towards Grandpa? [30]

It is a good joke, but just because it involves a real-life environment does not make it an authentic problem: authenticity should involve a real-life calculation and a consequence. (What have I learnt from the calculation, other than a number?) These are the component of authentic assessment from Ashford-Rowe and Brown [31]:

Authentic assessment
- is challenging. No-one is paid to do what has already been done or find out what is already known (to the employer), except perhaps as a rehearsal, or in a promotion interview. Thus, authenticity requires that the answer is either open-ended (hence undetermined) or genuinely unknown. Sometimes a little leeway is needed in interpreting this requirement. For example, students might be asked to play the role of expert witnesses in a mock trial, where the evidence is unknown to the court only in the context of the role-play (the academic staff having written the scenario).
- has a performance or a product as an outcome. This does not mean students might perform Maxwell's equations as interpretative dance. The product can be as simple as a written report, so long as the (authentic) audience for the report is specified. (More imaginative outputs are allowed.)
- is designed to ensure the transfer of knowledge. This is a challenge for the educational designer. It is easy to think up projects that will be treated

superficially. (If the answer to a calculation can be googled, why go to the bother of learning how to do the calculation?)
- has metacognition as a component. The authenticity often encourages students to reflect on their work as they might do in life, especially if they have to do something similar again.
- has a requirement for accuracy. This looks obvious, and in the sense that the outputs should not be erroneous it is; but it has to be interpreted appropriately. We do not expect first-year undergraduates to discuss the immune system (say) at the same level that we might expect of a professional immunologist. I have seen feedback that ignores this point, egregiously suggesting multiple opportunities for further exposition incompatible with the scope of the assessment. A completely correct answer is one that is as much as can be expected at the level of the student. (An intern might write a *first draft* of the president's speech and be judged accordingly.)
- has formal opportunities for discussion and feedback. I can see that the mastery of any skill requires a lot of practice of five-finger exercises and that dressing these up with context may be just clutter. However, exercises that have a point can provide intrinsic feedback. Asking students to consider whether a solution makes physical sense (in an authentic context) encourages them to think about whether their answer is correct and underpins a metacognitive stance.
- values collaboration. In life outside the examination room collaboration is rarely forbidden (except perhaps with a commercial rival). Students naturally collaborate anyway and this should be leveraged.

So, let us move on to some examples of authentic assessment.
1. Written essays and reports: Let us start with a common assessment—the essay or report. These have several possible purposes:
    - To teach elements of style and structure: in physics, the structure of a report is defined by subheadings (abstract, introduction, methods, etc), the mastery of which is obviously straightforward and requires little repetition. The style of a good abstract, introduction and so on is a high-level skill that takes time to acquire. When we try to teach these skills all at once students often make little progress. Better to take apart the elements and practice them one by one. We do not have to pretend that every report is a full research paper. When students do come to write a full report it will then be a more authentic experience of doing something they have been trained to do.

        My experience of student essays is based on a somewhat smaller sample than that of reports. I nevertheless believe that these too would benefit from authenticity in the same way, with one important distinction. As an authentic artefact, the scientific report has an implied audience beyond the instructor who is to mark it. The essay form, on the other hand, appears to cover a multitude of possibilities from an opinion piece in the popular press to an authoritative article in (say) the

New York Review of Books. The actual products seem to be none of the above, but a special category called the student essay, written for the marks. Essay mills exist to satisfy this demand. Some students may aspire to writing individual pieces for the *NYRB* or the *Economist* and their final year dissertation may reflect that. But, learning to write for a wider audience and to write collaboratively, as an authentic response in a problem-based approach, might be more relevant.

- To teach research and synthesis of material: the collaborative problem-based approach is also pertinent here. It addresses both essay mills and cut-and-paste from the internet. The problem of assigning individual marks requires a bit of thought, but the overall marking load can be reduced. (The length of the essay or report does not have to scale linearly with the size of the group.)
- To help commit material to memory: this is apparently the role of the traditional tutorial essay as preparation for the examination essay, as required also until recently by generations of school children. (Readers unfamiliar with school science examinations of 60 years ago may find it surprising that they required extended essays on such riveting topics as the extraction of aluminium.) The ready accessibility of such purely factual information nowadays means that the emphasis can be on finding, interpreting and using it. In fact, using information in a problem context engenders a need to know that makes it easier to remember.
- To develop communication skills: it is obvious that to develop communication we need to specify the intended audience. The exercise can then be authentic provided that the context is sensible. (This may seem obvious, but staff can get carried away.)

2. Asked to think of an alternative assessment, many instructors come up with a presentation. Instructors who have any experience of student presentations will come up with anything other than a presentation. The problems of assessing a few hundred student presentations should be obvious. The solutions are less obvious. One is the group presentation, which, for example, as a pitch, can be authentic. An alternative is an authentic conference. While some academics offer talks at conferences just to justify the travel expenses, most have something to say that the audience want to hear. This can be replicated in a student conference. For example, where a single group cannot obtain all the required data for an analysis and must rely on conference presentations from other groups, including assessments of reliability. We had student groups report partial observations of a simulated stellar light curve, and share their data to solve a problem. Another alternative involves student groups taking the lead in teaching certain topics. Other audiences include potential investors, philanthropists, line managers and awards committees.

3. If live presentations are difficult to schedule, recorded ones are an alternative. Most students have the resources to record voice-over PowerPoint or, even more simply, podcasts. Of course, these have to have an intended audience and, if the intended audience is the general public or other students, it is true that it is not possible to test technical details this way. But, it is surprisingly easy to recognise mastery of the subject from the extent to which the student struggles to fill the requisite five minutes: a lot of technical detail needs to be understood to give a convincing, simple and concise explanation of a difficult topic. Authentic examples include podcasts to accompany museum exhibits as well as more obvious contexts such as the *Economist* or *Science* magazines.
4. If it is more technical detail you want, then a website is a good place to require it. You need a problem context not just a topic, in order to ensure that copying Wikipedia is ruled out as an option for the students. One of my favourites is: How fast might it be possible for a human to run? Starting with the speed of light as an upper limit, the physics of heat transfer, and the biochemistry of metabolism and muscle make interesting content.

3.6 Authenticity and employability

A final aspect of alignment addressed by problem-based approaches is employability. Google searches reveal increasing attention to employability and attempts to define what it means. A review of the literature conducted for the Higher Education Academy found the subheadings (or scales) listed in table 3.2. These are not best addressed through a module on skills for employability, which lacks authenticity and results in weak engagement. A skills module is implicitly a deficit model. The

Table 3.2. The scales of employability, adapted from [32].

Affective:	
	Confidence, resilience and adaptability
	Experience and networks
	Behaviours, qualities and values
	Enterprise and entrepreneurship
	Self, social and cultural awareness
	Reflection and articulation
	Internationalisation
Psychomotor:	
	Career guidance and management
	Attributes and capabilities
	Specialist technical and transferable skills
	Knowledge and application
Meta-level:	
	Concepts and models
	Policy-related

key feature of this list of attributes is that it applies to a career within academia as much as outside. In other words, it is not a question of turning the academy into a vocational training institute; that would be to confuse employability with employment. Even further, the graduate attributes relating to employability are in essence the attributes relating to personal development; they are in fact, life skills. Such life skills are not acquired by exercises in box-ticking. It used to be implicit that a university education provided the scope for these in extra-curricular activities, and to some extent it still does. But, it is not helpful if there is a tension or disconnect between the perceived skills of the classroom (rote learning and examination) and the real purpose of education. Thus, I would argue that employability has to be built into the curriculum as a developmental process and that this is best done with some form of problem-based pedagogy.

To see this as a developmental process, we need here a taxonomy for the emotional attributes (the affective domain) and motor skills (the psychomotor domain) in parallel to cognitive taxonomies such as Bloom's (section 3.1). In fact, Bloom provided a taxonomy for each of the three domains [2, 33]. Since this is less well known, I will give a flavour here of the affective and psychomotor domains through a few selected verbs (one from each level). For the affective domain, we have

$$\text{acknowledge, comply, appreciate (value), compare (organise), discriminate.}$$

For the psychomotor domain, we have

$$\text{identify, react, copy, construct, adapt, create.}$$

This is too fine-grained for application to curriculum design; it is probably unrealistic to separate the individual levels, either meticulously or rigorously. So, something rough and ready might be a better guide. We use the three-stage student journey described by

$$\text{discover} \rightarrow \text{progress} \rightarrow \text{achieve}$$

or

$$\text{state} \rightarrow \text{explore} \rightarrow \text{apply}.$$

Note that these stages may correspond to the three years of a degree programme, but in general, they will not. We can now organise the HEA scales [32] in table 3.2, where each entry would have three stages. One might omit the meta-level entries as explicit components of design, rather thinking of them as applying to the overall process. In chapter 4, we will give an example programme.

To summarise where we are: In chapter 1, we looked at the drivers for change in university education and argued that to address these challenges we need to move towards thinking of the design of the curriculum as a whole. In chapter 2, we looked at the way students learn in order to examine the principal features of such a designed curriculum and settled on my view that it should involve a problem-based approach. We saw that such an approach covered a wide range of realisations in terms of the practical implementation of the pedagogy. In this chapter, we looked at learning outcomes and assessment, and we argued that problem-based approaches provide a framework for alignment between the pedagogy and the outcomes. In the next two chapters, we shall look at practical aspects of problem-based approaches.

References

[1] Bloom B S, Engelhart M D, Furst E J, Hill W H and Krathwohl D R 1996 *Taxonomy of Educational Objectives, Handbook I: The Cognitive Domain* (New York: David McKay)

[2] Anderson L W *et al* 2001 *A Taxonomy for Learning, Teaching, and Assessing: A revision of Bloom's Taxonomy of Educational Objectives* (New York: Pearson, Allyn & Bacon)

[3] Hussey T and Smith P 2002 The trouble with learning outcomes *Active Learn. Higher Educ.* **3** 220–33

[4] Adam S 2006 An introduction to learning outcomes (http://pedagogie-universitaire.blogs.usj.edu.lb/files/2013/03/An-introduction-of-learning-outcomes.pdf)

[5] O'Boyle E and Aguinis H 2012 The best and the rest: revisiting the norm of normality of individual performance *Personal Psychol.* **65** 79–119

[6] Donner Y and Hardy J L 2015 Piecewise power laws in individual learning curves *Psychon. Bull. Rev.* **22** 1308–9

[7] Ericsson A, Krampe K, Ralf T and Clemens T-R 1993 The role of deliberate practice in the acquisition of expert performance *Psychol. Rev.* **100** 363–406

[8] Kumamoto S-I and Kamihigashi T 2018 Power laws in stochastic processes for social phenomena: an introductory review *Front. Phys.* **6** 20

[9] Cousin G 2006 An introduction to threshold concepts (https://www.ecu.edu/cs-acad/writing/wac/upload/Intro-to-thereshold-concepts.pdf)

[10] Klaus A, Yu S and Plenz D 2011 Statistical analyses support power law distributions found in neuronal avalanches *PLoS ONE* **6** e19779

[11] McMillan D 1976 Sense of community: An attempt at definition Unpublished manuscript, George Peabody College for Teachers, Nashville, TN (quoted in [17])

[12] National Survey of Student Engagement (http://nsse.indiana.edu/index.cfm) (Accessed 20/9/2019)

[13] Australasian Survey of Student Engagement (https://www.acer.org/au/ausse) (Accessed 20/9/2019)

[14] UK Engagement Survey (https://www.heacademy.ac.uk/institutions/surveys/uk-engagement-survey) (Accessed 20/9/2019)

[15] Freeman T M, Anderman L and Jensen J M 2007 Sense of belonging in college freshman at the classroom and campus levels *J. Exp. Educ.* **75** 203

[16] Anderman L H and Leake V S 2005 The ABCs of motivation: an alternative framework for teaching preservice teachers about motivation *Clearing House* **78** 192 (https://www.jstor.org/stable/30189907)

[17] McMillan D and Chavis D 1986 Sense of community: a definition and theory *J. Commun. Psychol.* **14** 6–23

[18] Gibbs G and Simpson C 2004-05 Conditions under which assessment supports students' learning *Learn. Teach. Higher Educ.* **1** (available at http://eprints.glos.ac.uk/3609/1/LATHE%201.%20Conditions%20Under%20Which%20Assessment%20Supports%20Students%27%20Learning%20Gibbs_Simpson.pdf)

[19] Edmunds M 2008 Review of the student experience in physics (https://www.heacademy.ac.uk/system/files/physrev_final.pdf)

[20] Healey M, Flint A and Harrington K 2014 Engagement through partnership: students as partners in learning and teaching in higher education (https://www.heacademy.ac.uk/system/files/resources/engagement_through_partnership.pdf)
[21] Williams D P *et al* 2019 A framework for student–instructor partnerships (unpublished)
[22] O'Donnovan B, Rust C and Price M 2015 A scholarly approach to solving the feedback dilemma in practice *Assess. Eval. Higher Educ.* (https://doi.org/10.1080/02602938.2015.1052774)
[23] Saettler P 1990 *The Evolution of American Educational Technology* (Englewood, CO: Libraries Unlimited, Inc.)
[24] Keller F 1968 Goodbye teacher... *J. Appl. Behav. Anal.* **1** 79–89
[25] Rohrer D 2009 The effects of spacing and mixed practice problems *J. Res. Math. Educ.* **40** 4–17 (https://www.researchgate.net/publication/279601888_The_Effects_of_Spacing_and_Mixing_Practice_Problems)
[26] Broadfoot P *et al* 1999 *Assessment for learning: beyond the black box* (Cambridge: University of Cambridge)
[27] Black P, Harrison C, Lee C, Marshall B and Wiliam D 2004 Working inside the black box: assessment for learning in the classroom *Phi Delta Kappan* **86** 8–21
[28] Wiliam D 2011 Formative assessment: definitions and relationships (http://discovery.ucl.ac.uk/1507217/1/Wiliam2011What2.pdf)
[29] Donnelly R, MacPhee C and Bates S 2012 The performance gender gap in undergraduate physics (http://www.docs.hss.ed.ac.uk/iad/Learning_teaching/Academic_teaching/PTAS/Outputs/HEA_2012.pdf)
[30] Tipler P A 1999 *Physics for Scientists and Engineers* 4th edn (San Francisco, CA: Freeman)
[31] Ashford-Rowe K, Herrington J and Brown C 2014 Establishing the critical elements that determine authentic assessment *Assess. Eval. Higher Educ.* **39** 205–22
[32] Hooley T, Artess J and Mellors-Bourne R 2016 Employability: a review of the literature 2012–2016 (https://www.heacademy.ac.uk/system/files/resources/employability_a_review_of_the_literature.pdf)
[33] Bloom B S, Krathwohl D R and Masia B B 1973 *Taxonomy of Educational Objectives, the Classification of Educational Goals. Handbook II: Affective Domain* (New York: David McKay) (see also http://www.nwlink.com/donclark/hrd/Bloom/affective_domain.html)

Chapter 4

Implementing problem-based approaches

We now have the framework for implementing a problem-based approach, so we turn next to the practicalities. In this chapter, I shall look at these in general; in the next chapter, I shall look at physics in particular.

4.1 What is a 'problem'?

Let us remind ourselves what a problem-based approach is not. Traditionally, mathematical sciences are taught by lectures and follow-up problem sheets. Each problem sheet contains a number of exercises of varying difficulty that are designed to test the student's understanding of the lecture. In section 2.1, we saw one of the problems with this approach. Of course, one can design better end-of-lecture exercises, but these differ from a problem in the current sense, which is complex, offers multiple interpretations and comes at the start of the learning task.

A problem in this context is something that first of all engages the student's attention and drives a learning activity. This aspect is referred to as the *hook*. The problem provides intrinsic motivation. It differs from a research task (find out about a given topic because I am going to give you a test on it), which is extrinsically motivated. Students will need to know what to do with the problem: what they are going to produce as evidence of their solution. This is the *trigger*. Problem-based approaches are usually executed in groups because, as we saw in section 2.3, group discussions provide intrinsic feedback.

A problem should have a real-world aspect. Academia is part of the real world, we like to think, so a real-world aspect does not mean that the problem has to be 'applied'. But, the assessment then needs to be aligned with the real-world aspect and not just an exercise to create marks. The whole process can then be presented as authentic.

There is a further aspect of authenticity when we think of the development of professional skills. These too are embedded in the authenticity of the assessments as we spelled out in section 3.6.

Finally, the personalised aspect of the curriculum, which we discussed in section 2.9, arises from the open-endedness of the problem. While the problem may require core learning to be demonstrated, the scope can be made for the problem to be taken in various directions, for example, more highly mathematical treatments of more general cases, exploration of relationships to the research literature and so on.

Let us look at an example. I want one that is accessible to the non-physics community, so here is an example from an introductory module in neurophysiology.

Example 1: a problem like Maria

The Hook: this is given in figure 4.1. Here is an abbreviated version:

Ave Maria! We're of course talking about Maria Johnson, singer/songwriter/musician, on her whistle stop tour of the U.K. The multi-platinum, Grammy Award winner was in our back-yard, literally.

 Maria rose to fame after the release of her first album at the age of only 17. Her singing ability could bring rush hour traffic to a standstill, but it is her virtuosity on the keys that has sealed her meteoric rise to stardom.

Then came the moment everyone had been waiting for as she played the opening chords to her debut single, Unbelievable. The final song was worth the ticket price alone as it touched the hearts of everyone within earshot, bringing a fitting end to a wonderful evening.

Johnson, a Falling Star?

There were rumours that Maria Johnson had been feeling uneasy before the penultimate show of her sold-out U.K. tour, and these were only fuelled when the support act played on for a further 40 min. When she finally walked on the stage and began playing her signature debut track, it became clear from her stumbling and hesitant performance that something was horribly wrong, she seemed to have lost the fluency in the control of her fingers. She carried on, but eventually her band took over as she tried to compose herself. Being a committed live artist, who insists that none of her songs are mimed, she bravely battled on for two more songs before apologising to an arena full of confused fans and leaving the stage.

The trigger is given in figure 4.2. The scenario is described in the report that the students write

As a group, write a detailed report to Maria's GP regarding your evaluation of her condition, your final diagnosis and any treatment that you plan to give her. Remember that her GP is not a neuroscience specialist so you will need to explain the relevant neuroscience background where applicable.

As the two week (50 hour student workload) module proceeded, students were provided with additional results from the tests they recommended (sometimes called

Leicester Mercury

Ave Maria!

Judging by the sell-out crowd, it's little wonder that the second album sold as many copies on its first day of release as the first album had done in a week. We're of course talking about Maria Johnson, singer/songwriter/musician, on her whistle stop tour of the U.K. The multi-platinum, Grammy Award winner was in our back-yard, literally.

Maria rose to fame after the release of her first album at the age of only 17. Coming from a musical family, she plays several instruments, but came to prominence as an exceptionally gifted pianist in her early teens. Her singing ability could bring rush hour traffic to a standstill, but it is her virtuosity on the keys that has sealed her meteoric rise to stardom.

Then came the moment everyone had been waiting for as she played the opening chords to her debut single, Unbelievable. It is the mark of a great live musician that they can perform a track they've played on countless occasions and still make it sound fresh. The final song was worth the ticket price alone as it touched the hearts of everyone within earshot, bringing a fitting end to a wonderful evening.

Johnson, a Falling Star?

What a revelation it was when the young woman who could do no wrong actually left the stage half way through the penultimate show of her sold-out U.K. tour.

There were rumours that Maria Johnson had been feeling uneasy before the performance, and these were only fuelled when the support act played on for a further forty minutes.

When she finally walked on the stage and began playing her signature debut track, it became clear from her stumbling and hesitant performance that something was horribly wrong, she seemed to have lost the fluency in the control of her fingers. She carried on, but eventually her band took over as she tried to compose herself. Being a committed live artist, who insists that none of her songs are mimed, she bravely battled on for two more songs before apologising to an arena full of confused fans and leaving the stage.

Figure 4.1. The hook for a neuroscience problem as it might be presented to students.

Riviera and Sacha
Primary Care Trust

Patient Details

Name: Maria Johnson

NHS Number: 789 101 1121
Sex: Female

Date of Birth: 10 April 1987
Lifestyle: Musician

               Healthy, with no previous problems

Patient Symptoms/Concerns

- Experiencing irregularity in hand control that started with the middle finger of her right hand and has now spread to the fingers on either side of it.

- Patient first noticed the affliction a fortnight ago, whilst playing a musical instrument (piano).

- Patient has experienced minor headaches.

- No signs of physical/mental deterioration or injury.

Prescription:

Recommend rest and referral to specialists.

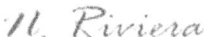

Figure 4.2. The trigger for the neuroscience problem (Example 4.1).

'dynamic PBL'). As implemented in the Natural Sciences programme, the problem had its flaws. The students get results only from pre-prepared brain scans and nerve conduction speeds, to which they are led. The original scenario specified a (very inauthentic) 3000 word report—presumably, the GP has an extensive attention span or time on her hands. It would have been better to ask students to write it up as a case study for a medical journal. This would also have had the advantage of guiding students naturally to the underlying science and providing a more realistic way of telling students if their diagnosis had been correct.

The student investigation was scaffolded with suggested reading for bi-weekly workshops, two sets of assessed 'end-of-chapter' exercises and two meetings with an academic neuroscientist (who actually wrote the problem). This is what I describe as problem-led tuition. We use the scaffolding to direct the students to the learning issues around fundamental science and away from the purely medical issues. In a medical degree, one might use the problem in a PBL mode in which the objectives were more naturally towards diagnosis.

The example does nevertheless illustrate what we mean by a problem in a problem-based approach. It also demonstrates that the problem-based approach does not specify how the teaching is to be implemented. The problem could be used at the start and end of a lecture-based course just to engage students and provide a framework for new knowledge. However, the group collaboration enables students from a variety of backgrounds to engage with the material, some new, some familiar, to different extents. Even though the diagnostic data was kept relatively simple for a first-year module, there was just enough uncertainty to force the group to engage in discussion. There is a correct answer to the diagnosis, but the report allowed students to focus to varying degrees on the fundamental science, but also on the clarity of the explanation. The module activity therefore embeds a number of professional skills and allows a certain amount of personalisation of learning. (There was also an examination that tested basic knowledge.)

Here is another problem which illustrates a much more open-ended approach.

Example 2: Nefertiti

To the editors of the New York Times:

Several claims have been made to have found the mummy of Queen Nefertiti, the latest of which will be broadcast on the Discoveries Channel on Aug 17. We at the University of [...] have obtained information from sources associated with the program to suggest that this association is less reliable than is claimed. We plan to carry out our own series of tests for which we would need your support, and would suggest in return that you publish our article on or around the time of the broadcast.
Yours sincerely,
Association of Sceptical Scientists

Students could suggest various approaches that this might trigger. These could include
- What scientific analyses could be used?
- What light does this discussion shed on the history of Ancient Egypt?
- What are the political or ethical issues around the funding and publication of scientific research that are thrown up by this case?

It is a good problem to allow students to define the curriculum; it needs some strong steering if it is to be matched to a pre-existing set of learning objectives.

So, can we generalise to what makes a good problem? As a guide, let us look at examples I have come across (and dissuaded potential users of) of some not very good problems. I have abbreviated the hook in all cases as this is not the issue.

1. You are asked to advise the government on the future of nuclear power taking into account energy requirements, potential technologies and safety.
2. You have been tasked by the government to review a drug prevention strategy for young people.
3. Build a crystal radio.

The first two are certainly stimulating, realistic and open-ended. In a Masters programme, they might be considered authentic, but then they are not really problems so much as titles for a report. In an undergraduate context (or the high school context from which they in fact come), they are not authentic: the government does not ask groups of students to review its policies, because students are in no position to acquire the necessary knowledge to do so. The idea that one can become an instant expert (government advisor) on subjects as complex as nuclear power or drug policy by googling a few websites is the antithesis of the aims of education. In the second example, I suggested that students look at the facilities available to young people on one particular housing estate (avoiding any contact with the drug scene). One can think of ways of narrowing the focus of the nuclear debate similarly.

The third example is an interesting activity for a hobby. Contrary to the aims of the originator, this would not teach anything about electronics. The internet is replete with circuit designs for crystal radios, together with lists of part numbers and where to order them. Students would probably learn more by building a model of a radio from Lego. To be a bit fairer, the original suggestion was to build a crystal radio to receive a radio station of the students' choice. But, the signal strength in practice gave no choice, other than the local radio station, which may have been the way of learning something, albeit a somewhat disappointing one.

So, here is a list (taken from an ITUE Delaware workshop) of what makes a good problem:

Requires professional working habits
Is open-ended and/or multi-pathed
Poses a stimulating question
Based on a realistic context
Complex (cannot be 'Googled' or guessed)
Encompasses several new areas of knowledge
Gives students a role or point of view
Encourages debate
Engages students
Leads to authentic assessment

We shall look at these in more detail [1]. (reprinted by permission of the publisher (Taylor & Francis Ltd, http://www.tandfonline.com)).

A PBL problem encourages professional working habits. The professional aspect of PBL is for us one of its main strengths and difficulties. The PBL approach attempts to create successful practitioners, not merely students successfully coached to pass examinations. In disciplines allied to professional practice, this is relatively easy. In medicine, there is a plentiful supply of medical histories of increasing complexity, which cannot be 'googled' and which can therefore be used as problems; in engineering likewise one can create problems of graded difficulty while remaining true to what a practising engineer might be expected to do. In physics, professional practice includes—indeed mainly revolves around—the physics laboratory. But, the real intellectual challenges faced by practising physicists are too complex to be used as vehicles for teaching: hence the widespread relegation of project work to the final year, once the student has 'learnt all the basics'.

It is very easy for students to tackle problems as amateurs, being satisfied with the first half-relevant thought as the solution. We have found ourselves inadvertently encouraging this by setting problems in contexts where one would not be expected to behave as a professional researcher. (For example, no-one abandoned on a desert island makes it a priority to keep a laboratory notebook. One is also unlikely to have a facilitator on the island. See section 5.2.) To repeat, the professional context for physics is a research team, and we have found it best that the problems generally keep it so. The content of problems is adapted to the level of the students, but the process is professional.

Our next desirable property for a problem, open-endedness, presents another issue. Most physics problems, as we currently teach the subject, are closed, in that the answer is either right or wrong. Educators who do not have any experience of physics have latched on to the supposed fact that, while there may be only one answer, there is more than one solution, that is, that problems can be tackled in a variety of ways. In my whole undergraduate career, I think I came up with solutions to exercises that were genuinely different from that expected and not just a superficially different presentation of the same solution, on at most two occasions. I do not think there is much mileage in requiring that PBL problems in the pure sciences should have multiple methods of solution, although there are some possibilities in experimental design work. Our approach is to require the problem context to be such that the answer has consequences, for example, where the range of outcomes using different values for unknown quantities might affect a decision. Instead of being provided with values for various quantities, students are asked to estimate them using information from various sources which might give different results. As an illustration, a rough estimate of the ability of the UK national grid to support the replacement of petrol with electric vehicles gives a very debatable answer dependent on the assumptions made.

A PBL problem poses a stimulating question in a realistic context. In strict implementations of PBL, a problem should pose a question, not a mission statement or an instruction to do something, as one might find in a project. This is relatively easy in medical education, where the real context of a problem is authentic and accessible, even if some doctoring of the source material is required. In pure sciences, at the opposite extreme, an authentic context for an accessible problem is often impenetrable at the current stage of the student's knowledge, or just so much clutter. We have seen how in the light of this difficulty a number of variants of PBL have arisen that we have characterised as problem-based pedagogies.

Nevertheless, the issue is sometimes misunderstood. In solving a problem in, say, classical mechanics, a student might be expected to look up and have to learn, say,

Newton's Laws. This is something that no practising physicist would need to do and for many teachers this makes the problem-based approach appear artificial. But, it is no different in kind from the experience of the medical student who has to look up some basic anatomy. The skills that a student will employ in coming to grips with a problem involving classical mechanics are the same collection of research skills that a professional researcher will employ on more advanced material. In addition, once we expand our horizon beyond the pure discipline, we can find many questions in environmental science, biophysics, geology and so on that provide problems in physics at all levels.

PBL problems encompass new areas of knowledge. Many academic staff think that they get the point of a problem-based approach as an aid to reinforcement or revision. But, 'they can't solve that because we haven't taught them this yet' is a common complaint about other uses of problem-based pedagogies. Actually, PBL is a great aid to reinforcement, even where this is not the main motivation. It is also true that there is only so much new knowledge that can be incorporated in a single problem. But, there should be something new that students recognise that they need to learn.

A problem gives students a role or point of view. Giving a point of view is important and difficult. Students are not experts, so problems that attempt to provide a role and a point of view by stating 'you are an expert in climate change …' are confusing. Constructing the learning issues becomes a tortuous navigation of the response that 'if we were experts we would know that'. Often the source of the difficulty is the context. Students are unlikely to be researching basic geology if they 'work for an oil exploration company', but they might be if they are doing some archaeological research. One of our most problematic was 'you have been selected to advise a Hollywood production company', which, for some reason never clear to the instructors or students, was a company interested in being lectured to on the correct science for their science fiction movie set inside the human body. (Great perhaps for introductory biology, but you need only a superficial knowledge of biochemistry to advise the animators on appropriate representations.) For the most part, we find that most academic staff (and students) are more comfortable if we dispense with the pseudo-roles and just treat students as fellow professionals, essentially as a research team with a line manager. The point of view should be implicit in the problem. If the problem really is to measure the speed of light, there had better be a reason why we should not just look it up.

A problem should be engaging. This is again where a lot of the effort in constructing a problem-based programme comes in. We find that students are readily engaged by what they can easily already do, but this defeats the object. On the other hand, if it is too difficult it is not engaging (at least, not beyond the initial encounter with the prospect of, say, computing trajectories through gravitational wormholes.) An engaging problem is one that it ought to be possible for students to solve with just the right amount of effort allowed for in the schedule. An engaging problem should also be one appropriate for group work. Two obvious sources of failure are problems which neglect to recognise resource limitations (only one set of vital equipment, for example), so end up being done by a sub-group, or which clearly lend themselves to horizontal division. (Each group member learns the statement of one of Newton's laws, or of one welfare theorem.)

I shall look at some examples from physics in chapter 5.

4.2 The learning cycle

In practice what makes a good problem will be constrained by other aspects of the programme: the length of a module, the timeframe, class contact opportunities and so on. So, we shall look at these in the following sections. Common to all implementations, however, is the learning cycle. It is easiest to explain this by an example. Perhaps the most widely known is the Maastricht Seven Steps, so we shall use this:

Step 1. Locate the problem: in groups, discuss the hook and make sure everyone in the group understands the problem. Identify and clarify unfamiliar terms presented in the scenario; a scribe lists those that remain unexplained after discussion. The problem is not always obvious to students even if it is to the instructor. The Maria problem above is a good example: the facilitator will need to guide students to a fundamental understanding rather than a medical diagnosis. A short period of silence, while students read the problem (even if this has been provided in advance), is helpful to allow all students to formulate a contribution and avoid the more forceful students dominating the discussion. A scribe records an agreed statement of the problem as understood by the group in their own words.

Step 2. Identify the questions that need to be answered to make progress with the problem. Define the problem or problems to be discussed; students may have different views on the issues, but all should be considered. A scribe records the problem statements.

Step 3. Identify (without evaluation) what the group already knows that might contribute to potential solutions to the problems. Suggest possible explanations on the basis of prior knowledge; students draw on each other's knowledge and identify areas of incomplete knowledge. A scribe records the discussion. There should be no evaluation at this stage—all ideas should be considered. This can be done as a class exercise with the various groups contributing to a class list.

Step 4. Analyse and structure the results of the previous discussion. Review steps 2 and 3 and arrange explanations into tentative solutions; scribe organises the explanations and restructures if necessary

Step 5. Formulate learning objectives and a course of action for the knowledge that has been identified as lacking. The group reaches consensus on the learning objectives. The tutor ensures that the learning objectives are focused, achievable, comprehensive, and appropriate.

Step 6. Carry out an independent study using articles, books, practicals and lectures to gain the required knowledge. In private study, all students gather information related to each learning objective. The tutor (or scaffolding) ensures that students each do all the research and not just a part of it.

Step 7. Discuss the findings and repeat. The group shares results of private study (students identify their learning resources and share their results). The tutor checks the learning and may assess the group.

We employed a slightly different version for a time:
1. Locate the problem and identify the questions
2. Existing knowledge that can be brought to bear
3. Identify the learning issues thus raised
4. Course of action to be agreed
5. Enquiries and/or experiments to be conducted, leading to new knowledge, skills or resources
6. Share results amongst the group
7. Theorise and
8. Evaluate progress against target
9. Reflect and repeat

Although it is generated from a mnemonic, it is not exactly memorable. A shorter version might be:

> Formulate the Problem: Decide the Learning Issues:
> Do the Research: Evaluate progress: and Repeat

The important point is that we have a learning cycle, even if the problem is completed within a single one hour session.

4.3 Scaffolding problem-based approaches

The key differences between implementations of problem-based approaches occur in the way in which the steps of the learning cycle—the identification of the learning issues, the following actions and independent study—are managed. There are two aspects to the management: the organisational issues, which we shall take up in the next sections, and the tutorial support which we consider here.

The way in which students are supported in a problem-based curriculum is the crucial key to successful implementations. The support structure is usually referred to as scaffolding, a term introduced in [2] to refer to the way in which instructors respond flexibly to students' difficulties and progress, fading the level of support through time so that responsibility for learning is transferred effectively to the students [3]. A lot of the resistance to problem-based approaches seems to arise from a misunderstanding of the degree of scaffolding that can be provided at each stage, while still employing a problem-based pedagogy. Let us consider some of the steps of the learning cycle from the point of view of scaffolding.

Learning issues: In PBL, guidance on the immediate learning issues may be provided by the instructor (facilitator) in response to group discussion and may range from a gentle steer to a specific instruction. More generally, in problem-led tuition, guidance on the learning issues may also be provided through specified preparatory reading or discussion questions for each session. Guidance may also be given indirectly through the specified learning objectives which, in the extreme, can be provided on a session-by-session basis.

Group work: it is sometimes assumed that students are endowed with the ability to work in groups, or if not, will learn on the job. This is frequently not born out by the evidence. Thus, group behaviour needs scaffolding. This can be done through induction, with the formulation of group rules, and observation of behaviour by the instructor, and some procedure for when there is a breakdown in group function.

Facilitation sessions: Groups are usually expected to meet on their own outside class time to some extent, but the extent to which an instructor (facilitator) will be present is part of a decision on the degree of scaffolding. If facilitation involves workshop sessions, the instructor may choose to make important points raised by a group available to the whole class, or even to run the workshop as a series of questions with groups reporting on each in turn. Usually, towards the end of an extended problem, the groups will be expected to meet more often without an instructor in order to formulate their response to the problem.

Research: students may be instructed on general principles and resources available. More generally, there may be a reading list or lectures (and computer or laboratory practicals) either alongside the group work or aligned to particular steps in the problem, or as preparation for specific group sessions. Students may be directed to use group sessions as preparation for lectures from academic staff (in which student questions to the lecturer could form a major part). There may be exercise sets to provide technical skills or to reinforce basic knowledge, including multi-choice computer-marked questions. Feedback for these exercises can be given in various ways: written, small group tutorials, whole class or peer-marked.

Output: Scaffolded support for skills is as important as support for subject knowledge. If the output is, say, a report then guidance on extended writing will be provided as part of the scaffolding. In a curriculum constructed by design, such support will be faded over the course of the programme. Similar remarks apply of course to other forms of output.

One of the major issues in implementing problem-based approaches is getting the scaffolding right. In my experience, it is never a process of selecting an off-the-shelf structure. What works is dependent on the discipline, the students, the staff and the physical environment. Appropriate scaffolding is part of design science whereby pedagogy is responsive to feedback. It is unusual to get everything right first time.

4.4 Managing problem-based approaches: shapes and sizes

For the management aspects, we need to consider the structure of the programme. Problems can be posed within a single class session, or there can be one or more problems covering a whole course or module. If students are expected to do their research between class sessions, then these have to be scheduled accordingly, or the research load managed correspondingly. The frequency of instructor contact will be related to the degree of scaffolding in the sense that research on the learning issues must be appropriate to the time available between meetings, taking into account students' other commitments. The choice of group size and the mode of formation will be linked to the timescale and mode of facilitation. Students need 'student-time' to complete assessments remembering that student-time is not only much longer than the equivalent staff time, but much longer than the time that staff imagine it to be. (Staff also need marking time, but that requires less of an imaginative leap.)

Figure 4.3 shows two aspects of problem-management, which we have called shape and size, some of which are illustrated in our previous examples.

Missing as a potential shape is the closed end-point, closed path, since this is not in the spirit of problem-based approaches. Short problems can be introduced into lectures or workshops (as they often are in staff-development sessions). If the research step involves consulting the lecture notes, then the single class session can encompass the whole cycle; otherwise, students can be encouraged to bring their research to the next session. The opportune introduction of problems into a lecture-based course can be a way of transitioning from lectures to a problem-based approach over time. A problem-a-day has been the approach used in Singapore Polytechnic. At the other extreme, we often used a single problem for each module of our Natural Sciences programme over a six week period. Practitioners generally argue against multiple problem-based activities in parallel and hence do not favour multiple long thin problems at the same time. Some implementations (for example, i-Sci at McMaster) involve a series of problem-based or project activities alongside more traditionally lectured modules. There are many examples of a single module (or no more than a few modules) with relatively loosely defined content objectives, designed primarily for the skills content. We give some examples of possible stand-alone problem-based modules in examples 7 and 8 and section 5.2 of chapter 5. None of these structures work if they are not planned around the students' actual workload, that is, unless the programme is designed from a student perspective.

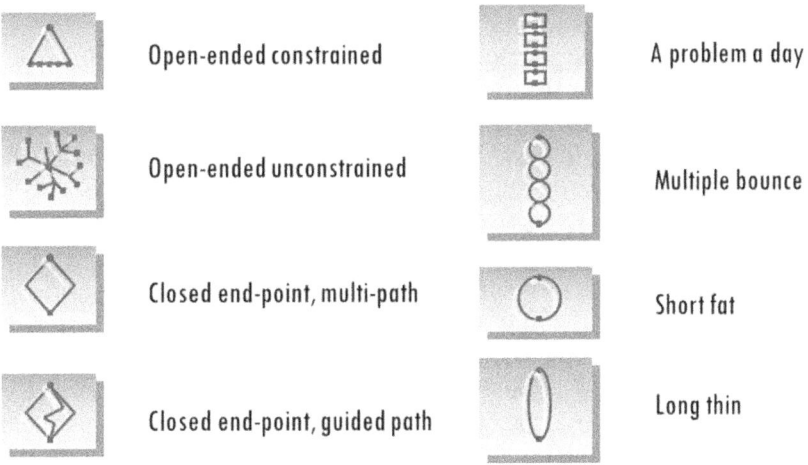

Figure 4.3. Shapes and sizes of problem-based approaches.

Delegates to our workshops have often found a planning template useful. A simple form will contain the following information:
  Subject Area
  Topic
  Year/Level
  Class Size
  Group Size
  Time to Run
  Problem Summary
  Problem Description
  Learning Outcomes

To this, we need to add the management structure, which we consider next.

4.5 Managing problem-based approaches: facilitation

Students require support throughout the process of problem-based tuition. Support for group work is usually provided through teacher–group interactions referred to as facilitation. The use of the term facilitation is intended to indicate that the teacher provides guidance to the group research, not the answers to all of their questions. This is hugely confusing both to instructors and to students. 'I'm not allowed to tell you the answer to that question' is rightly regarded by students as unhelpful. This is not facilitation, since it obviously does not facilitate anything. Nor does 'Well what do you think?' A guide to facilitation and facilitator training can be found in, for example, [4–6]. My basic rule is that the facilitator leaves the group only when the students have a clear idea of what to do next.

There are various ways of providing facilitation. With a single instructor, there is not much choice: the instructor moves from group to group in a class session. This is referred to as the floating facilitator. In the structure where issues for discussion have been set by the problem-designer, I like to get groups to share information by reporting out to the class.

If there is more than one facilitator available, they can be fixed or floating. A fixed facilitator will take a group through the problem in multiple sessions. As far as the group is concerned, this is their only facilitator, but the facilitator may have more than one group. It is possible for a fixed facilitator to manage groups of a larger number of students than the floating facilitator. Typical numbers for floating facilitation are 4–6, whereas a fixed facilitation group can number as many as 12 students.

An advantage of a fixed facilitator is that sessions become more like good tutorials, with everyone having a stake in the outcome for the group. The disadvantage is that they can become more like bad tutorials, with the facilitator leading the discussion as if it were a lecture. A problem-based approach does not obviate the need for effective instructors by re-labelling instructors as facilitators.

The fixed facilitator model is the one developed for medicine, where it seems to work. With guidance from the facilitator, students complete each meeting having formulated the issues they need to study in order to make progress and come prepared to the next session. I do not think it works so well (or at all) in the physical sciences and mathematics, because there is a higher barrier to formulating a sensible course of action. Basically, students have an insufficient idea of what it is they do not know in order to formulate a set of learning issues. (How would you know that you needed to study quantum mechanics to interpret a spectrum if no-one told you—or told you the reference, which amounts to the same thing?) This leads to superficial research, where the first googled search that turns up what looks like it might be an answer in less than a page constitutes the work for the next session. This is one of the drivers for the more detailed scaffolding we discussed in section 4.3. A disadvantage of the floating facilitator is obviously the division of time between groups.

4.6 Managing problem-based approaches: groups

Group sizes and group formation is a contentious issue, much researched [7, 8]. Some instructors like randomly assigned groups. This may work with a relatively homogeneous cohort, or if the problem is more about skills than content. I personally cannot make it work where the class is widely dispersed in ability (or work ethic). A compromise is to keep top and bottom sets together and mix the rest. The ability measure here should be based on performance in individual assessments, not on group assessments; otherwise, the bottom groups at any one time are subsequently fixed and demoralised. The problem with poor performance is usually more a question of work ethic than ability. With group membership based on individual performance, students who think they are better than their current group have the opportunity to demonstrate this by putting in the effort. Conversely, in the usual case where the number of students is not divisible by the desired group size (or even when it is), we would usually make the lower groups larger to give them (in principle) more people power.

In the 'how to' literature a group size of an odd number is often recommended to avoid splitting into equal halves, and hence to discourage any subdivision at all. The literature also contains various recommendations for the frequency with which groups should be reassigned. There are no established rules. Natural breaks occur between problems, between modules, between semesters, and between years and there are arguments for and against each. With this, as with scaffolding, the only approach is to see what works.

One other major problem with groups we have already mentioned is the distinction between teams and groups. While we want students to work in groups, some students seem to work as teams. For example, in a group all the members learn the four equations of Maxwell. In a team, they can divide the laws between them, one each. This is clearly not as intended. In part, this is addressed through the design of the problem, in part through scaffolding, and in part possibly not at all. It is probably fair to say that, in practice, any actual division of labour would not be as extreme as of such collective entities as Maxwell's equations; selective, strategic learning in problem-based approaches is probably no more prevalent than question-spotting for examinations, and for most students, a lot less.

Students do not generally arrive with an existing ability to work effectively in a self-organised group. Some instructors manage this by assigning group roles, for example, chair, scribe, timekeeper. Some instructors reinforce these roles by assessing them and providing feedback or even marks. Most give this up after a cost-benefit analysis. We have tried giving each student a simple engagement mark (for example, 0, 0.5 or 1) on the basis of active participation in the group. This conflicts with the support role of the facilitator. In theory, that is with sufficient resources, one could employ an independent observer to provide a group mark. In Finland, I found this role played by a group member who is tasked with providing and recording feedback on the group performance in each session (although not a mark). Of course, the group roles rotate between meetings.

Probably more effective (although not exclusive) is a group induction session. This involves getting the group to set their own ground rules in writing, particularly in attendance and the recording of meetings. Students are often required to work together as a group on their own outside classes. In the early stages, the instructor can drop in on these meetings (by arrangement) to observe and advise.

With any group work, problem-based or not, there is the ever-present issue of problem groups and students for whom working in a group is problematic. Problems within groups require the intervention of the instructor. Students with special needs should receive special support to help with group participation, but this requires special resources. As a last resort, we have occasionally arranged for students to work more on their own, or give them an individual assessment. In one extreme case, following advice from our student support professionals, and with the agreement of the student and the (admittedly reluctant) agreement of the class, a student was moved between groups for each fortnightly problem, so that no group worked with this student more than once. The problem is solved (that is, removed) by abandoning group work, but therefore also eliminating a key feature of the problem-based approach, to the detriment of most students.

Finally, we shall discuss staff training for problem-based approaches in chapter 6. As you might guess, most implementations use a problem-based approach for this, so that instructors can experience for themselves some of the difficulties (and benefits). In an ideal implementation that really followed the research student–research supervisor model, the instructor would learn to solve the problem along with the students!

4.7 Managing assessment and feedback

Finally, we return to the starting point: learning outcomes and their assessment. The issues specific to problem-based approaches are group related. Some implementations attempt to assess the group behaviour as a group, either through real-time observation, or minutes of meetings, or other records of activity. Some examples I have seen attempt to assess the performance of individual students in group roles. A fixed facilitator might have time to note the levels of engagement of the group members, but even then it is unclear whether the time processing this information is worthwhile. I have always found combining the role of facilitator and performance marker awkward. (Assessing objectively if a group has done a calculation correctly is another matter.)

On the other hand, my experience of group workshops in which there is in fact a mark for content is that students are much more focussed on the tasks. A possible alternative is an element of competition. The point is not just the in-workshop activity, but the incentive to do the preparation.

One criterion might be that students have to turn up to their group meetings (both class and self-organised) to get the full group mark for the deliverable (unless of course there is a valid reason for absence). This introduces another dilemma: do you provide the answers to the learning issues? That is, what do you do with a group that is struggling? In the medical context, it is clear how to steer students to the correct diagnosis, and hence to achieve the required learning objectives.

But, here is a harder example. How long can you safely leave a dog in a car with the windows closed on a hot day? On the web you can find various conclusions, but not the arguments behind those conclusions. So, we need to guide students to set up a mathematical model, and solve a differential equation of a novel type, either approximately or numerically (so there are a range of acceptable answers and approaches). We can assume that students have studied differential equations, have had a class on mathematical modelling and have researched heat and radiation (the designated learning outcomes). Some students will start by arguing whether the breed of dog they are dealing with makes any difference and delve into dog anatomy. The facilitator can probably deal with that. Then they argue about the thermal conductivity and albedo of the different materials (glass, metal, painted metal, cloth, leather), how large the windows are, the colour and type of covering of the seats. Perhaps the facilitator can suggest they simplify the model without actually telling them to consider a glass cuboid. Suppose they now spend a lot of time failing to set up an *ab initio* model. Is there perhaps something similar they can use to short circuit the process? Anything? ...What about the greenhouse effect? There, you've just given away the point of the problem, or much of it. But, with a struggling group, this is just what I would do (or at least where I would try to lead them).

The mark for the final product or deliverable is in principle awarded to the group. Some instructors ask students within a group to award marks to the other group members (or sometimes including themselves), with possibly a fixed total to distribute. These marks can be used for scaling, provided that they make sense (i.e. are not too diverse). All of these are ways of implementing peer review. There is often a reluctance on the part of students to differentiate between contributions, until they reach some critical level of divergence below which the marginally contributing student gets marked down unfairly heavily. If most students agree equal shares, that cuts down the workload required to check peer reviews. Where there are (significant) differences one can require them to be supported by other evidence. We require contemporaneous records of meeting attendance, and of the fulfilment (or otherwise) of agreed tasks in order to support negative peer reviews. The process is a lot simpler now we have electronic media for record keeping.

One interesting and unexpected outcome of peer review is that students are intolerant of, and quite good at spotting plagiarism by other group members, usually where odd words have been changed from an internet download in a last-minute attempt to fulfil the group agreement.

4.8 Managing change

A discussion of implementation would not be complete without some consideration of the management of change. I shall discuss this a little more fully in chapter 6 when we consider staff attitudes to problem-based approaches. Here I make some initial observations.

Many of the implementations of problem-based approaches are led by individual enthusiasts, often following the employability agenda. (See section 3.6.) The reader will know by now that I do not believe these work in general. (Exceptions occur where there is a clear rationale for the different module structure, for example, in workplace-related projects, where the external involvement provides a good reason for the difference.) Even when they do work (when, for example, the problem-based activity is not high stakes) they are vulnerable to changes in staffing.

The main argument, however, is that differences between modules should reflect solutions to issues with those modules. A free-standing problem-based module should not be one person's solution to problems that remain unaddressed in other courses. So, managing change means first identifying problems. The impediment is that the large changes in pedagogy, such as we are discussing, require large problems to gain traction. Some of the initial ventures into PBL were instances of major problems, including issues of recruitment and retention, or where institutions starting new programmes wanted or needed to be seen to offer something different. In theory, such institution-wide change can be implemented from the top down by fiat, especially now that academic tenure is less secure than in the past. There are now many institutions with experience for an aspirant to draw on (Maastricht, Aalborg, Delaware, etc).

Most institutions, however, do not have (or do not believe they have) such existential or large scale problems. This leaves us with the scale of the Department or programme. I believe there are three vital components, apart from the identification of a problem. These are a de-facto teaching team, external validation and funding. In proposing a team, I do not mean that several academic staff should individually introduce a problem-based approach into their own modules (although done coherently that would be a start). I mean that a team can argue with colleagues for change more effectively than an individual. One way might be to introduce a new problem-based activity taught by the team perhaps as a pilot project. Where this has been tried as an individual initiative, it has often failed to grow, whereas team-based initiatives tend to gather more momentum. External funding helps in two ways. First by paying for the resource to implement change, either as bought-out teaching time or the employment of assistants to help with the development work. Second, by itself acting as a source of external validation, something which can be more important than the relatively small sums of money involved. Finally, external validation can be achieved by involving external experts in the planning—consultants who can speak with some authority on educational matters—and in the evaluation. This last is especially important when things do not work out exactly as hoped, not because you will not be able to see the problems for yourself, but because the external voice can also promote the positives.

Finally, change is pointless unless it is cost-effective: we shall look at the costs in chapter 7 and the outcomes in chapter 6.

4.9 Putting it together: an example

In [9], we constructed a number of case studies, synthesised from real examples, in order to illustrate some of the points we have made. Since this is readily accessible, I shall not repeat these case studies here. I shall, however, add one real example of our Natural Sciences programme at Leicester. In the period 2007–19, this three or four year programme was delivered exclusively to classes that grew to typically 20–30 students. More recently, the programme has been amended to reduce the amount of teaching exclusively to natural sciences students, and to include modules from other science programmes with added problem-based components. In this, it resembles somewhat the i-Sci programme at McMaster. The following account is adapted from [10] and describes what is now the problem-based core of the degree programme rather than its totality. I shall also omit many parochial details such as changes in the length of modules.

The core programme in Natural Sciences is delivered by what we have called problem-based tuition. Each sequential five or six week core module begins with a problem or a research question. For example, for the first module:

The ancient Greek historian Herodotus wrote that 'Egypt was the gift of the Nile'. You are commissioned by a publisher to write an article discussing this in a scientific context.

This is a problem only in the sense that students need to first elucidate its meaning; it is really a research prompt. Students investigate how much of what the Ancient Egyptians knew of astronomy, biology, chemistry, geology and physics can be related to modern science. They are provided with an academic essay of 3000 words, in the style of a research paper, which they have to unpack. This introduces students to all the disciplines over five weeks, at an introductory level for those new to a particular subject, and in a novel context for those who already have some background. It also provides an example of how to write an essay.

Students are supported by a handbook of about 50 pages. This contains a detailed list of learning objectives and an overview of the topics for each of the twice weekly facilitation sessions. For each of these sessions, there is detail on the preparation required, including questions to think about and preparatory reading. The questions are there to help students to read intelligently, as well as to seed the discussion in the facilitations sessions. Thus, the class preparation is somewhat more scaffolded than is usually understood in PBL, where students are asked to identify for themselves the learning required to address the problem [11]. It comes closer to a written version of the verbal guidance one would expect a graduate student to receive from a supervisor, except that it lays out the whole module in advance. Some of these questions are straightforward; some are conceptual; others might simply ask students to think about the relevance of their reading to the module problem. There is some evidence for the claim that this level of scaffolding, through what are effectively worksheets, or their close kin, is either counterproductive or neutral with respect to student performance in problem-based pedagogy [11]. Although we have not carried out a formal analysis, our impression is that it provides confidence in the programme for the stronger students and a clear exposition of what is expected of them for the weaker ones.

Students have one two-hour and one one-hour facilitated workshop each week, working in groups on the questions with a floating facilitator. There are two lectures each week from subject experts to which students are encouraged to come with questions. We refer to these as 'expert sessions' to emphasise the intended interactivity; we draw on research expertise from about 50 academic staff across the University. There is also a weekly set of exercises to be completed individually and submitted electronically for marking. The more straightforward exercises are peer-marked at the weekly class tutorial, while the longer ones are tutor-marked. For the purpose of peer marking, the questions are broken into parts that each carry marks of 0, 1/2 or 1, and a couple of submissions are randomly checked by the tutor each week to guard against collective cheating. Marks for these exercises count towards the module mark to a (very) small extent. There are a few variations from this structure. The first week of a module starts with a class session 'brainstorming' the problem, locating the problem and thinking about the learning issues. This activity provides an overview of the module. The final week has no classess, allowing students to work in their groups on the submission of the essay. Figure 4.4 shows the scaffolding in diagrammatic form.

Alongside the core module, we run a skills module. This differs from a bolt-on skills module in that the skills are related to the core current at the time. So, for the first module skills would include, for example, literature searching, referencing, basic writing and plagiarism. We also include how to read a textbook intelligently, especially reading mathematics, which is unfamiliar to some students. These skills are tested in the core module, not separately. But, the essay is marked for style and content, with the style mark contributing to the skills module mark, and only the content mark to the core module. There is an examination that contributes 35% of the overall module mark.

The journey to this structure was a long one. For the first five years of the programme, the structure was changed every year. We experimented with group formation (eventually settling on streaming according to performance on individual work, with some minor adjustments, for example for gender balance. For the first module, we also try to have groups with a mix of science backgrounds from physics, chemistry and biology, since most students will not have all three.) We experimented also with frequency and length of facilitated worskhops. Meeting once a day proved counter-productive as students satisfied themselves that a few minutes googling something to say constituted a day's work. In truth, two hours is slightly too long for a session, but an hour proved too short and submultiples cannot be timetabled. The

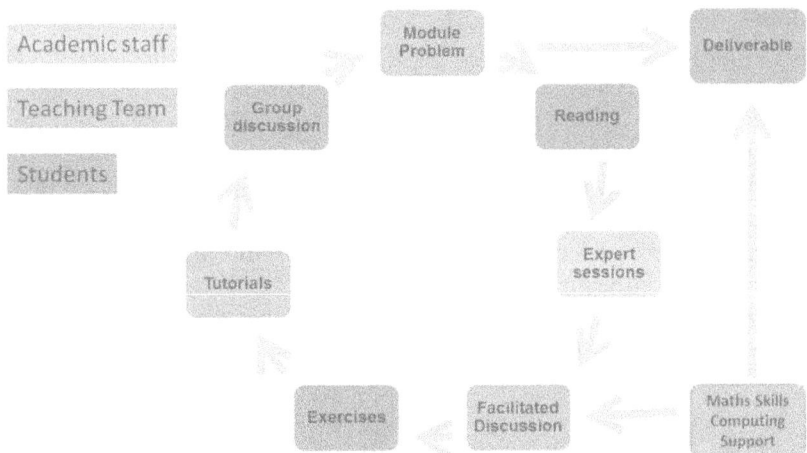

Figure 4.4. Scaffolding problem-based tuition.

shorter second session of the week was initially dictated by resource constraints, but actually proves to be generally sufficient. The weekly homework grew out of various attempts to get students to study the reading in appropriate detail. The use of peer marking of homework was again a resource issue, but serendipitously proves to be a valuable activity [12]. The listing of preparatory reading would not be essential now that we employ specialist teaching fellows as instructors (and facilitators), but initially provided some quality control for sessions that were led by casual staff (mainly PhD students) in the early days of the programme.

In the initial development of the programme, we made use of post-graduate and post-doctoral facilitators in classical PBL mould. This did not work well, despite training and support, largely because these external contributors have no ownership of the programme. (Although it never got to the point that Schmidt [13] describes of facilitators taking their knitting to the sessions.) For most of the life of the programme, we have instead employed a dedicated teaching fellow (in effect, and now in practice, a lecturer with a teaching mandate only) in each of biology, chemistry, physics and geology [14].

In the early days we tried to run laboratory classes in parallel with the core modules, and in fact some of the early problems involved practical and theory, but the limited availability of other peoples' laboratories and other scheduling issues made that impossible. So, there is now a separate laboratory programme in physics, chemistry and biology for all students, as and when the relevant laboratories are free.

The skills module includes a weekly problem set in mathematics, related as far as possible to the core content taught by a version of mastery learning as described in section 3.4. We tried initially to teach this by problem-based tuition on the grounds that this would make it more interesting. But, in fact, that added an unnecessary burden for students. However, in response to student requests to put more emphasis on the uses of mathematics, we introduced some additional 'applications' questions, which could add to the module mark, but were not required to pass the weekly submission. Finally, all modules apart from the first give students the opportunity to submit an extension piece of work for additional credits, either on a suggested topic or an agreed topic related to the module. The submission can be in a format of the student's choice: report, essay, podcast, voice-over powerpoint or poster. It provides an opportunity for enthusiastic students, provided they have completed the core to a satisfactory standard, to take further a subject that interests them. This has produced some interesting pieces of work, including a course handbook for a short problem-based tuition module on quantum computing!

For the whole of the life of the programme the teaching team has met once a week to exchange information, both about current issues in teaching and recruitment, reports on progress in developmental work, and opportunities for research and attendance at forthcoming conferences. There are also two one-day meetings a year of the core team to chart major developments, and a general yearly update open to all staff involved in the programme. In the beginning, pastoral support was provided by academic staff from across the contributing departments in a not very effective manner. Subsequently, once they were in post, pastoral care has been provided by the core teaching team, delivering a greater sense of community for the natural sciences cohort.

We have evolved here a long way from pure PBL where we started. This evolution arose from feedback, both explicit (several rounds of externally conducted evaluation) and implicit (our experience of what works). Evolution is not deterministic and is strongly environmentally dependent. Thus, implementing problem-based tuition is a journey and not an event. The starting points will be different, as the examples in the previous chapter make clear. But, so too will be the stage points and the endpoints, except in regard to the positive benefits to students.

References

[1] Raine D and Symons S 2012 Problem-based learning: undergraduate physics by research *Contempor. Phys.* **53** 39–51

[2] Bruner J S, Wood D and Ross G 1976 The role of tutoring in problem solving *J. Child Psychol. Psychiat.* **17** 89–100

[3] Volman M, Beishuizen J and van de Pol J 2010 Scaffolding in teacher–student interaction: a decade of research *J. Educ. Psychol. Rev.* **22** 271

[4] Duch B J, Groh S E and Allen D E 2001 *The Power of Problem-Based Learning* (Sterling, VA: Stylus)

[5] Azer S A 2005 Challenges facing PBL tutors: 12 tips for successful group facilitation *Med. Teach.* **27** 676–81

[6] Kolmos A, Du X, Holgaard J and Jensen L P 2008 Facilitation in a pbl-environment (www.euronet-pbl.net/wp-content/uploads/2009/11/Facilitation_in_a_PBL_environment.pdf)

[7] Fonteijn T H H and Dolmans D H J 2019 Group Work and Group Dynamics in PBL *The Wiley Handbook of Problem-Based Learning—Wiley Handbooks in Education* ed M Moallem, W Hung and N Dabbagh (New York: Wiley) pp 199–220

[8] Blumberg P 2019 Designing for effective group process in PBL using a learner-centered teaching approach *The Wiley Handbook of Problem-Based Learning—Wiley Handbooks in Education* ed M Moallem, W Hung and N Dabbagh (New York: Wiley) pp 343–66
[9] Raine D and Symons S (ed) 2005 *Possibilities: A Practice Guide to Problem-based Learning in Physics and Astronomy* (HEA Physical Sciences Centre) (https://www.heacademy.ac.uk/system/files/ps0080_possibilities_problem_based_learning_in_physics_and_astronomy_mar_2005.pdf)
[10] Raine D 2015 *Innovative Practices* (York: Higher Education Academy)
[11] Choo S S Y, Rotgans J I, Yew E H J and Schmidt H G 2011 Effect of worksheet scaffolds on student learning in problem-based learning *Adv. Health Sci. Educ.* **16** 517
[12] Gibbs G and Simpson C 2005 Conditions under which assessment supports students' learning *Learn. Teach. Higher Educ.* **1** (available at http://eprints.glos.ac.uk/3609/1/LATHE%201.%20Conditions%20Under%20Which%20Assessment%20Supports%20Students%27%20Learning%20Gibbs_Simpson.pdf)
[13] Schmidt H 2007 *Plenary lecture delivered at the International Problem-Based Symposium Changing Perspectives on Problem-Based Learning—Reinventing PBL* (Singapore)
[14] Gretton S, Raine D and Bartle C 2014 Scaffolding problem based learning with module length problems *Conf.: European Science Education Research Association Conf. 2013* http://doi.org/10.13140/2.1.2156.4162

Chapter 5

Problem-based physics (and other disciplines)

Most instructors find that getting to grips with the writing of problems for problem-based tuition is hard work. Potential problems turn out to be too hard, too easy, too googleable, too closed, too open, not to address the learning objectives, too long, too short, etc. It takes time to develop a problem. In the first section, I present some ideas that can help. I will then go on to discuss problem-based pedagogies in the laboratory. The examples have all been chosen from my own experience, so that I can use them to illustrate particular aspects of implementation.

5.1 Sources of problems

Problems developed by other instructors can be found on the web in various repositories, although these are dominantly at the high school and college level, and web searches bring up broken links where sites have not been maintained. The Institute for the Transformation of University Education (ITUE) at the University of Delaware is one of the oldest and has useful links [1]. While problem-based approaches are widely used across Medical Education and increasingly so in Engineering (where the University of Aalborg is a world-leader), this is less so in other disciplines, particularly outside the professions. (The University of Maastricht is a well-known exception). In higher education in physics, examples of institutions that use problem-based pedagogies to a significant extent include the University of Delaware, Dublin Institute of Technology, and the Universities of Portsmouth and Leicester, and the University of Edinburgh uses flipped learning. Closely related pedagogies, such as Peer Instruction under Eric Mazur at MIT, and at Stanford under Carl Wienman, are widely used in the USA in courses for freshmen. However, even if they are accessible and at the right level, because they are context-dependent, problems usually require adaptation; but they can be a source of inspiration.

Articles in newspapers and other media can be sources of ideas, and occasionally even discipline research can suggest a problem. Problems can be presented in text, as photographs, audio, video or even as physical objects. Alternatively, we can start from existing exercises and turn them into problems. In this way, it is easier to develop problems that cover the intended learning outcomes, so we shall start with an example of this approach.

Example 1

Here is a step-by-step example of the development of a problem from an-end-of-chapter exercise (adapted from [2]). I have omitted some details because the point is to illustrate the different levels of scaffolding, not to solve a physics problem. The problem is based on a current astronomical discovery that just happened to provide a novel way to cover some existing learning objectives. We shall start with the discovery, and see how it can be framed as a standard exercise or as a guided problem.

> Ultima Thule is a Kuiper Belt object imaged by the New Horizons spacecraft. Ultima (figure 5.1, the larger lobe) and its counterpart, Thule, are primordial building blocks from a time when smaller objects called planetesimals were merging to form the planets we know today. Computer simulations suggest that the two objects that make up Ultima-Thule collided at a speed of just 2-3 m s^{-1} [3].

The first step is to identify the problem. Students cannot reconstruct the computer simulation, but they can be led to calculate the sort of tumbling motion that would be compatible with the quoted approach speed. For this, they will need some data. The first piece of information needed might be identified as the mass of the two objects. This cannot be obtained directly, but it would not be difficult to find the size of the object. So, to get its mass, students need the density of the material it is made of. Here are three ways of providing this:

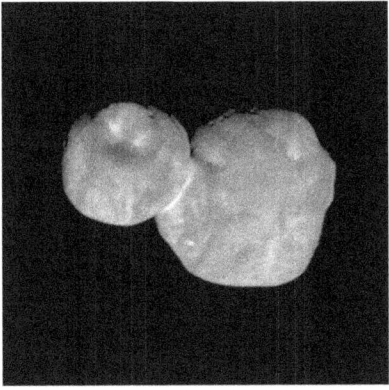

Figure 5.1. The Kuiper Belt object Ultima Thule. Credit: NASA/Johns Hopkins University, Applied Physics Laboratory/Southwest Research Institute [4].

(i) The density of the object can be taken to be 3000 kg m^{-3}.
(ii) You may assume that the object has the same density as porous rock meteorite.
(iii) Make an estimate of the density of the object based on the information above, and any other sources you care to use. (Reference your sources in full.)

The first of these would be the way information is provided in a standard closed exercise, in which all the necessary data is provided, and nothing given to the student is redundant. The disadvantage is that the numerical value involves no judgement; it could be anything. In any case, how would it be known? The second offering prompts the students to estimate the density, but does the generalisation for them. The third way obviously requires more work on the part of the students, but is more rewarding in that they learn something about meteoritic material.

Next, we might ask students to make a model, again in one of three ways:
(i) You may model the asteroid as a dumbbell consisting of two spheres separated by a rod. Use the parallel axis theorem to work out the moment of inertia of each sphere of the dumbbell about the centre of mass of the dumbbell (midway along the rod).
(ii) Make a simplified mass model for the object, e.g. a pair of discs or spheres or some combination of these. Hence deduce a value for the moment of inertia about an axis passing through its centre of mass.
(iii) Estimate the moment of inertia of the object.

Again, the first is the way we would do this in the standard problem sheet: all necessary information is given and the student has to demonstrate an ability to use it. But, all the hard work has been done: the problem has been reduced to looking up the formulae in the textbook. This is very often the easy part of a physics problem: the hard part is making a model that is sufficiently simple to be calculable, and sufficiently close to reality to be worth calculating. The third version leaves it to the student to work out that a simplified model is required. Of course, we would expect that students will have had some practice in doing this, or will receive some tutorial guidance.

Following on, we might ask students to look at the collision. Once more we can look at three different ways of doing this:
(i) You can assume that the collision is inelastic and that the asteroids adhere to each other after the impact. Use the conservation of linear and angular momentum to compute the motion of the combined object after the impact.
(ii) Would you expect the collision to be inelastic or elastic? Stating clearly any simplifying assumptions you make, describe the motion of Ultima Thule after the impact.
(iii) Describe, as quantitatively as you can, the motion of Ultima Thule after the impact.

Notice that the results the students obtain here will depend on their modelling at earlier stages. The problem is open-ended in that there is no one right answer (although of course there are an unlimited number of wrong ones). Different groups may adopt different levels of sophistication, but they will be assessed for the consistency of their proposed solutions. Whatever calculation they actually do, if it is correct, it will involve the same physical principles, and hence cover the learning objectives.

Finally, we could turn the whole problem into the basis for a problem-based approach by putting the problem at the start of the process as in figure 5.2.

I have updated the original problem (used in the physics programme at the University of Hertfordshire), which involved the collision of an asteroid with the Earth and was presented in a dynamic scenario.

Example 2

Here, in a rather more condensed form, we jump straight from an end-of-chapter exercise to the problem-led version. You do not need to follow the details of the exercise to appreciate the point. First the problem in the form of an end-of-chapter exercise:

(a) A coil of length 10 cm, radius 1.5 cm has 1000 windings. What is its inductance?
(b) Calculate the capacitances for two tuned LC circuits, frequencies 160 kHz and 500 kHz using the inductor in part (a).
(c) A parallel plate capacitor has a plate area of 10 cm^2. What plate separations are required to obtain the capacitances in part (b)?
(d) What is the Q-value of a circuit with $L = 10$ mH, $C = 1$ μF and $R = 1$ kΩ.
(e) What resistance placed in series will be required to ensure the two signals are separated in the tuned circuits of part (b)?

The Sunday Reporter
NASA's New Horizons Reveals Geologic 'Frankenstein'

Ultima Thule is a Kuiper Belt object imaged by the New Horizons spacecraft. Ultima (the larger lobe) and its counterpart, Thule, are primordial building blocks from a time when smaller objects called planetesimals were merging to form the planets we know today. The two spinning objects that now make up Ultima-Thule collided at a speed of just 2-3m/s. The rotation rate of the combined object should give scientists a clue on the initial spins.

XXXXXXXXXXXX

Full story p8

Figure 5.2. A hook for a problem in rotational dynamics.

And then in a problem-based approach:

.... The sugar is well mixed into the liquid cocoa using our Melangeur. Both the sugar and cocoa solid particles are ground down smaller and smaller, while more and more fat is released from the cocoa. The sugar/cocoa mixture becomes smoother and remains a thick liquid known as chocolate 'paste', now ready for the refining and conching process to follow [5].

From the documentation, it is clear that the control of the size of sugar particles is important in chocolate manufacture. The Grenada Chocolate Company is a small company in the Caribbean which might benefit from semi-automating the grinding process. To do this, is it would be necessary to check the granularity of the sugar being introduced to the mix. A simple way to do this would be to design a circuit to measure the bulk dielectric constant of the granulated sugar, and to give an audible warning if this falls outside an acceptable range.

Resistance to problem-led approaches from academic staff comes to a large extent from the impression that it applies to introductory physics, and not to the more advanced content that they teach. To address this, I want to present three problems from more advanced topics: electromagnetism, quantum theory and general relativity.

Here are two problems that together provide an attempt, which we shall critique, to teach Maxwell's electromagnetic theory. In section 5.2, we shall present these problems in their original context as laboratory practicals. Here we consider just the theoretical aspects.

Example 3

Problem 1: The Atlantic Cable [6]

21 August 1858:
Since the year 1842, when Professor Morse ...first commenced his series of experiments in the laying of submarine cables, the idea of an Atlantic telegraph has never slumbered. On the 10th of August, 1843, Professor Morse wrote to the Secretary of the Treasury: 'The practical inference to be drawn is, that a telegraph communication may be established across the Atlantic. Startling as this may now seem, the time will come when this project will be realized'.

28 August 1858: Complete Success of the Atlantic Cable.
The telegraph cable is a complete triumph. Messages are passing over its wires quite freely, and there is no doubt a short time will enable our electricians to increase the velocity of transmissions so as to bring it up to those already in use. It is needless to remind the public how few had faith in such a wonderful achievement a month ago....

Students were given an extract from [7] about the history of the Atlantic cable which we will not reproduce here. Instead, here is the trigger:

The year 2008 will be the 150th anniversary of the first Atlantic cable. A public demonstration lecture at the Royal Institution will mark the occasion. You have been commissioned to construct this demonstration lecture of the principles involved, which must provide clear explanations and supporting mathematical calculations as well as descriptions of experiments. You will be given data from a number of experiments to work on.

Problem 2: Sand in the desert:

The Big Idea plc has been commissioned to study ways of searching for leaking water pipelines in the desert. The pipes are either on or near to the surface, so any leaks would result in wet sand in the vicinity. However, it has proved difficult to detect this reliably by photographic means, since dark shadows can also be caused by dunes, vegetation, clouds, etc as well as by wet sand. The research department has decided to investigate the possible use of drones carrying equipment to measure the dielectric constant of sand, under the assumption that this will change with the moisture content. A number of ways have been considered to measure the dielectric constant, specifically the (i) Brewster angle and (ii) the reflectivity of the surface in the microwave, infrared and optical bands, and data has been obtained for each approach.

The first problem is authentic only in so far as the calculations of the properties of transmission lines were argued over at the time. But, they can now simply be looked up and in any case would not feature in a public exhibition. One might note that, unknown to us when we set it, it turns out that the second problem is a method used by engineers to assess the water content of concrete, but students would not have been helped by discovering this. Used in a physics context, however, its authenticity is dubious. In physics, Maxwell's theory is used to explain how light can be treated as an electromagnetic wave. Once we have this piece of bookwork, calculations tend to be about the propagation of waves. But, a problem-based approach to the propagation of waves (as in leaking pipes) then does not involve Maxwell's theory! (So, it has to be shoehorned in.) The issue we have to solve is to make Maxwell's equations themselves central to a problem. If we were teaching electrical engineers, this could be straightforward. We might, for example, pose a problem of aerial design. But, this is not something that would be amongst the learning objectives of a physics programme. Next, then is a problem that I claim really does involve an understanding of Maxwell's theory, and furthermore is based around current research.

Example 4: Peter Pan's shadow

If Peter (a very small person) wears a cloak that bends light through an angle greater than the angle of incidence his shadow will disappear. Is such a cloak in theory possible?

The following paper will provide a background to the problem...[students are provided with material on transmission lines and a simplified account of negative refractive indices].

In the problem of Peter Pan's shadow students need to explore the structure of Maxwell's equations, and what they say about the interaction of radiation and matter. I should add that we found it necessary to steer students away from worrying too much about the exact shape of the cloak, and particularly the fabrication of negative refractive index materials. The latter can be readily googled, but that does not help with understanding the fundamental physics at the appropriate level. Strictly the relevant material can be fabricated only in two dimensions, whereas the calculations are only simple enough for a one-dimensional material. But, on the positive side, this does cover the same learning objectives as our cable (transmission lines) and leaking pipes (reflection and refraction) as well as Maxwell's equations.

So, perhaps the sceptic will accept that we can use a problem-based approach for electromagnetic theory, but what about modern physics—relativity and quantum theory? The following is a problem that does both, based on an approach to general relativity by Morris and Thorne [8].

Example 5: quantum theory and relativity

Area 51 Briefing Document.
The following document has been obtained from MI6 files.

Additional information on Area 51 (Roswell UFO) TOP SECRET RESTRICTED CIRCULATION Additional information on Area 51 (Roswell UFO) (redacted) xxxxxxxxxxxxxxxxxxxxxxxxxxxxxxx examination of partially charred material within the crash zone appears to indicate an expected journey time of three months xxxxxxxxxxxxxxxxxxxxxxxxxxxxxx designation of the home world as zeta (2)-Reticuli xxxxxxxxxxxxxxxxxxx advanced wormhole technology xxxxx

Initial investigations concluded that this was part of a hoax to discredit the US military. The physical limitations on near light speed travel, even allowing for the effects of special relativity on proper time, were thought to rule out any nearby star for the alien host planet. However, recent advances in technology (especially GPS systems) have verified the importance of gravitational effects on time dilation. Exploratory studies in general relativity have failed to rule out the possibility of wormhole structures in spacetime that might be constructed by an advanced civilisation having access to negative energy matter, despite the paradoxes that appear to arise by allowing travel into the past.

Students are asked to produce a technical report on this issue. Scaffolding was provided in the form of guided reading and code templates, in the symbolic algebra software Maple, to calculate proper time, embedding diagrams and verify solutions of Einstein's equations.

Quantum theory was introduced through a follow-on problem as to whether the alien visitation could involve teleportation. This brings in the Hilbert space structure of quantum mechanics. It leaves out the traditional approach of separating variables in the Schrödinger equation to obtain (with some use of 'it can be shown that' when it comes to applying the boundary conditions) the structure of the hydrogen atom, something which students think they already know anyway.

Here is another way that we can take advantage of current research, to get away from the traditional heavy emphasis on the teaching of quantum theory on solving differential equations, to an application of the simplest model of a quantum particle in a box:

Example 6: quantum dots

Breakthrough: The Internet Gateway to Today's Great Discoveries.
By Reg Derrick—our China Correspondent.

Quantum dots (QDs) as fluorescent probes have found increased applications for cell labelling, tracking of cell migration, and *in vivo* imaging. Magnetic nanoparticles also show many advantages in biological applications (for example, as a new type of magnetic resonance imaging contrast agent). Now, it seems we can put the two together. A recent report [9] has shown that Fe_3O_4-CdSe nanoparticles exhibit both fluorescence and superparamagnetism. Illumination with UV light produces visible fluorescence from the CdSe, with a size-dependent wavelength, and allows us to track the particles; magnetic control of the ferromagnetic Fe_3O_4 core allows us to move the particles to where we want them. We can then zap them with a magnetic field to destroy any cancer.

Students were asked to write about the science behind the Breakthrough report, which is highly inauthentically circular given the origin of the report. A better problem might be based on the size dependence of the bandgap in semiconductors to engineer fluorescence at different wavelengths.

So far, we have looked at multi-path problems with fixed endpoints. I shall end this section with two, more open-ended approaches. Both of them are directed to a persistent criticism from employers that students may be able to speak knowledgeably on some advanced topics they have recently studied, but are less able to recall some basic science and use it in problem solving.

Example 7: physics challenge

At one time, long before modularisation was even a word, students used to sit a synoptic examination at the end of their programme. This was a chance for instructors to set hopefully interesting problems that might cross course boundaries. Interesting questions usually make for hard examinations, and it is indeed surprising just how difficult it is to answer unseen problems on a mix of topics under examination conditions. Our physics challenge module is designed to give students practice outside the examination. Students tackle problems in groups, prepare solutions, and present their answers as pairs of groups in a challenging environment. A facilitator picks a member of each group to answer a problem in turn. The other group can challenge for additional points (translated into marks using an algorithm that takes account of the number of problems presented by each team in the time available). While a group can obviously share the preparation work amongst the members, because they do not get to choose who presents, they need to be certain that all members understand all the solutions. The competitive element appears to ensure that a class solution does not circulate amongst the groups (or perhaps they are just very honest). There are also enough problems that those selected vary between years. Students do not get given possible correct answers, except that facilitators are asked to point out egregious errors if these are not challenged. (Examples of these problems can be found in [10].) Students generally engage with the course work, although the examinations still produce a much wider range of outcomes than taught modules.

Example 8: Journal of Special Topics

In section 2.6 we saw various ways in which the research process can be embedded in the curriculum. Missing from this in most undergraduate programmes is the experience of a research scientist as the creator and publisher of content. To some extent, the research apprenticeship of a final year project fills part of the gap. Students may also be told about peer review and form some idea of how science works, but still absent is the experience of finding a problem, and taking it through the peer-review process. Finding a tractable problem is probably the most difficult aspect of academic research, and seeing it through to appearing in print is the most exhilarating. We want our students—all of them, not just those going on to PhDs and research careers—to experience this.

The *Journal of Special Topics* is an activity for physics students at Leicester in their final undergraduate Masters (MPhys) year. The basic idea is that students write short (one page) papers on topics of their choice. They submit to the journal, which has an editorial board, the composition of which rotates round the class. Their papers are sent to other members of the class for refereeing (peer review), and the editorial board decides to publish or not, or require revisions, on the basis of the referee reports. Students may work in groups, or alone, on both the papers and the refereeing task.

Students are assessed through the number of papers published (really authentic!) and the number of reviews (less authentic), with the final average mark scaled to the overall class average in order to derive a percentage mark for the module. There is some oversight by the staff of published papers to ensure that trivialities, or obvious howlers, are not being awarded marks (although in the real world erroneous papers do get published).

Students meet weekly with a facilitator for help with developing ideas. There are also seed papers written by the staff. In the early days, students used to base their ideas on these seed papers quite closely. In recent years, a trend has emerged in which students attempt to find novel contexts for analysis, and there is now a stock of past issues of the journal to consult for inspiration.

The electronic journal software is the free OJS publishing system, so the finished product looks entirely professional. We also produce a paper copy for students as a souvenir using a self-publishing web site. Although never intended to be in the public domain, the contents of the journal do appear in search engines. This has led to some publicity for some of the more intriguing papers. A paper entitled 'How much of the Amazon rain forest would it take to print the internet?' is one example of several that have appeared in the national media.

Some of this attention has been adversely critical and initially sent shock waves through the University. ('Why are students wasting time on this nonsense?') In fact, as a learning exercise it fulfils several unique functions. It provides a forum for creativity, not only in solving problems, but in coming up with problems to solve. Students think up problems that they then try to model as best they can. This opens the door to genuine discussion. (With luck, final year research projects can provide the same opportunity for problem solving, but usually without the publishing process.) Thus, students also learn first-hand about peer review (and its limitations). They learn to respond to criticism (including when it is not justified), which provides an opportunity to develop resilience. And they learn to think critically about work they are not familiar with. They also learn how hard science is if you do not know which module (if any) you are being tested on!—and, concomitantly, how well you need to know something to be able to draw on it out of context. Finally, and this is the hidden agenda, students get to revise basic science from years one and two in a context which is not patronising (even if for some it is a little intimidating).

There is also a version of the journal in the natural sciences programme at Leicester, which is international in the sense that students at McMaster University, one of our student exchange partners, can receive credit for papers submitted to the Leicester journal as part of their writing assignments. (They are subject to the same refereeing process.)

5.2 Laboratory PBL

My first experience of developing PBL was in the physics laboratory. This was a purely tactical choice in that the idea of getting away from the traditional scripted experiments was supported by the staff who ran the laboratories. At the time, PBL in the laboratory was unusual if not unique in physics (where PBL was in any case unusual), although, as we saw in chapter 2, it had been adopted in project- and problem-based engineering programmes, and there were also examples in chemistry laboratories. Our first example of PBL in the laboratory illustrates some of the challenges.

A desert island problem

Desert island rescue problem

> You are the crew of cargo plane carrying goods for a large industrial wholesale company. Whilst travelling through a storm your plane is forced to make a crash landing on a small isolated island. Most of the equipment on the plane has been damaged by the landing and only a few rudimentary components remain useable. Air traffic control knows you are missing but does not know where you are. You therefore need to build some kind of rescue beacon. [Students are provided with a list of equipment salvaged from the plane. The list includes two rescue beacons but no power sources.]
>
> You begin to explore the island. Your survival situation doesn't seem too bad: there is plenty of fruit and seafood to hand, and the climate seems balmy with a pleasant sea breeze to keep you cool. Water was a problem at first, but you've discovered a type of vine which yields freshwater when cut. You're left with the issue of being rescued. How can you attract attention? If only you could find a way to power those rescue beacons ....

Now, spot the mistake! It turned out to be the mention of fruit. The intention was to direct attention away from survival (food and water were not a problem) towards the availability of wind power (the breeze). But, students come to a problem with prior knowledge, being in this case more familiar with the lemon-powered batteries they made at school than with the construction of wind turbines. The laboratory technicians were inundated with requests for lemons. (A journey to the local supermarket was made to provide them, if only so that the students could discover for themselves the need for power not voltage.) In any case, as a laboratory practical the scenario fails the test of authenticity. For example, no-one 'abandoned on a desert island' makes it a priority to keep a laboratory notebook, or to estimate their experimental errors. One is also unlikely to have a facilitator on the island.

The learning objectives, which include Ohm's law, potential dividers, capacitive circuits, can be met in a different way as illustrated by this extract from the Otherton News:

> Crosswinds are Critical:
>
> Another incident this week serves as a reminder for pilots to consider crosswinds on approach to land. Bob C's Puffin Aerosport suffered minor damage after a gust of wind affected the aircraft on landing. Bob was approaching runway 27 (due west), with air traffic control reporting wind from the northwest at 21 knots. The Puffin is rated for crosswind components up to 15 knots, so Bob went ahead with his landing, only to be caught by a gust on touchdown. The plane veered onto the grass at the side of the runway and

bent an undercarriage leg. The airport emergency team arrived at the scene quickly, but Bob was unharmed and able to exit the aircraft unassisted. He intends to have the Puffin flying again within three weeks.

This is the second incident this year involving crosswinds. Pilots are advised to read the operating manuals for their aircraft to determine crosswind limitations and operating procedures. When on approach, they monitor the wind information given by air traffic control and keep an eye on the windsock to assess gusting.

Asked if anything was being done about this state of affairs a spokesperson for Otherton Airport management said that they would be pleased to receive ideas for a safety beacon, but that this would have to get CAA approval.

This version has a distinct advantage that it is not the actual beacon that is to be constructed, but a scaled-down model. Students therefore have to calibrate their device (by assuming some relation between wind speed and output power), which requires some attention to the theory intrinsic to the problem.

Wet sand revisited

The remote determination of the wetness of sand that we discussed above (problem 2 of example 5.3) was also used as a laboratory problem. I discuss it again here because it illustrates several points.

In the laboratory practical version, each group is assigned two experimental set-ups to measure reflectivity (one in each waveband), one in each of two laboratory sessions. Each group has access to either dry or wet sand (but not both), so will therefore need to share results with other groups. This is the first point. Since any one group will not carry out the complete suite of experiments they will need to obtain information from the other groups in order to reach a conclusion. Each group presents its findings at a meeting. Groups then have to decide their recommendations to the research department as to which, if any, of these methods they would advise them to pursue further.

Reports are assessed on the quality of the arguments in support of the conclusion. The conclusion in itself is neither right nor wrong, except in as much as it is supported by correct arguments. This is the second point and a quite difficult one to get across. Part of the project involves writing a computer program to show the theoretical reflectivity as a function of angle for different levels of water saturation and to compare this with the data. Sometimes the data is too noisy to make that comparison, but some students will still identify one small bump (amongst many) at around the angle they expect, as giving them the Brewster angle. I do not see that the experiment has failed if the conclusion is that the data does not fit the theory. In fact, it provides the opportunity not only to understand the importance of honesty in science, but also to think about why the data might not fit. (One exceptional group did investigate the distribution of the sizes of the sand grains on the reflectivity of the surface, instead of treating it as text-book smooth!)

The problem as I have presented it appears to attempt to integrate laboratory practicals and theory. This is quite hard to get right. If the equipment works perfectly, and the experiments amount to no more than collecting data that is the same every time, then why not just give students the data? If we have a genuinely interesting experimental set-up, where the data is noisy and needs to be interpreted, this produces cognitive overload for students not thoroughly versed in the theory, so the experiment becomes an add-on. I do not claim that it is impossible to get this right, only that it is problematic. In fact, we separate the theory and practical, so the problem is presented first as theory and only then as a laboratory investigation. We also separate out the instrumental skills component of practical work, so that, as far as possible, students are familiar with the equipment they will use in the investigation of a problem.

5.3 Induction

But, to return to the beginning, students need an induction session. For practical work, this will involve some low stakes problem-based experiment. I shall give this one in full (apart from some management details):

UltraKleene

UltraKleene is a new stain-removal fluid that the manufacturers say is more penetrating than its competitors. The Advertising Standards Authority (ASA) has received several complaints about the claims made in UltraKleene's advertising campaign and has asked your laboratory to look into the matter.

The ASA has already informed UltraKleene Corp that their marketing claims are under investigation. The company has responded by sending a laboratory report supporting the assertions made in the advertisements. Your task is to report as to whether the representations made in the UltraKleene advertisement are fair.

Students are provided with supporting material including the video of the advert in question (made in house by my two teaching assistants) and the following: letters of complaint received by the ASA, a report from the UltraKleene Corp. (reproduced below), and an extract from an article on diffusion [11].

A comparative investigation of penetrative power of ULTRAKLEENE and the main rival cleaning fluid
Abstract
This investigation proves that ULTRAKLEENE cleaning fluid is superior to rival cleaning fluids in terms of its penetrative power. It is clear from the results herein that ULTRAKLEENE consistently out-performs competitors in this sense: it takes ULTRAKLEENE 45–60 s less than competitors to be imbibed into sample blotting paper over a distance of 4 cm.

Introduction

In the competitive market of cleaning fluids, the penetrative power of the product (the rate at which it is imbibed/absorbed into the target material) is a key factor in the products ability to act quickly and effectively to soak and clean. These experiments were carried out in aid of proving ULTRAKLEENE to be the number one cleaning fluid in this sense. If the absorbency times were faster using ULTRAKLEENE than rival products, then it would be clear to see that ULTRAKLEENE is superior and more penetrative.

Discussion

A large number of tests were carried out to characterise the flow rate for both ULTRAKLEENE and the main rival product. The tests comprised of taking measurements of the time it took each fluid to penetrate to a particular height into blotting paper. A single type of blotting paper was used for consistency. Testing over short scale lengths is appropriate in terms of the scales involved in everyday stains.

Results

The graph (figure 5.3) plots the progress of ULTRAKLEENE fluid up the paper strip as a function of time. An average was taken of the performance of our rival cleaning fluid and this is plotted against the progress of ULTRAKLEENE.

Conclusions

The results graph clearly shows that in all tests the performance of ULTRAKLEENE is better in terms of penetrative power. The flow of both ULTRAKLEENE and the rival cleaning fluid seem to follow power laws of the form:

$$L^\beta \propto t$$

where L is the distance to which the cleaning fluid has progressed into the absorbing material in a time t. The exponent, β, for the relationship governing the flow of the rival fluid is clearly less than the exponent for the relationship followed by ULTRAKLEENE, indicating the flow of ULTRAKLEENE is progressively quicker than that of the rival.

The activity is run over one afternoon with groups of four students. Student groups have their own bench space, which contains basic equipment (stopwatches, rulers, multimetres, etc) so there is some (limited) choice in experimental design. The outcomes of this activity were always illuminating. The first thing to say is that there is no difference between the two fluids. (They are both coloured water, and the results shown from repeated trials were simply assigned to the two fluids post hoc.) Nevertheless, the experimental results will always show a difference. This is because it is difficult to get accurate results: the differences are due to experimental error. Thus, no sensible conclusion can be made unless the plots of the data include these experimental error bars. Nevertheless, the majority of groups find that ULTRAKLEENE is superior. The correct conclusion is that the scientists at StainZap were somewhat sloppy in their experimental design, and the reporting of it, and too conservative in their error

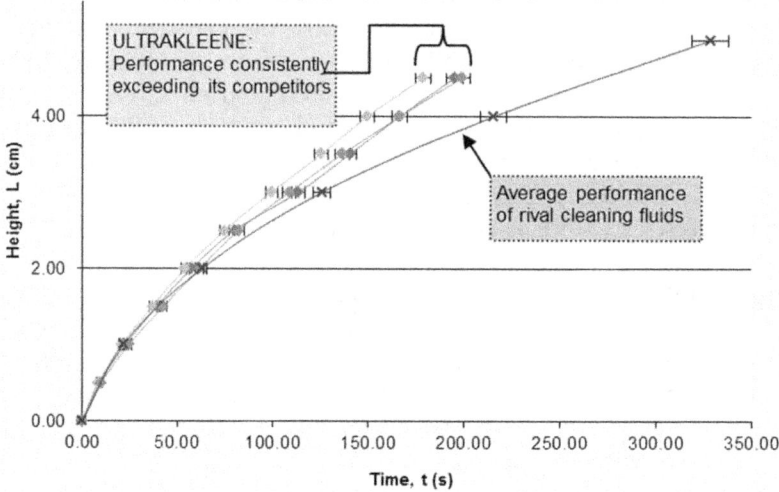

Figure 5.3. Velocity curves illustrating the rapid rise of ULTRAKLEENE in comparison to the average rival brands.

estimates. (In fact, the practical is not about diffusion rates, but about documenting procedures and estimating errors.) This leads to a discussion as to whether the scientists were guilty of malpractice or incompetence, or simply seeing what they thought they were paid to see. How would we know? Probably we would look at the evidence in their laboratory notebooks. So, what would we find if we were to look at your (the students') notebooks for the afternoon …? Finally, did MI6 really believe that Iraq had weapons of mass destruction?

This problem involves a sufficiently simple experiment that it can be used as a general introduction to problem-based tuition. It is important that students become familiar with the process in a low-stakes context, particularly the group aspect, but also with what is in some cases for them the disorienting absence of only one correct answer.

5.4 Other disciplines

Education for the professions is an area where problem-based tuition is a natural approach because, as we have seen, the professional context provides an authentic alignment between aspirations, outcomes and learning. Pure sciences are less easily seen as candidates for a problem-based approach, because the professional research agenda of the instructors is so far removed from the technical apprenticeship required to access it. But, physicists do get to date religious artefacts and advise on light levels in historic buildings; chemists get to test for heavy elements in water supplies and look at the yields of industrial syntheses, so problem-based scenarios that develop basic science are not hard to find.

An area of commonality between physics and other disciplines is the trend towards collaboration, as seen in the increasing average number of authors on research papers [12, 13]. This lends authenticity to the notion of working in groups in those disciplines.

Away from the sciences, the arts and humanities widely adopt the academic apprenticeship model, with extended essays as the main learning activity. In most, if not all, students are required to access the primary literature, the essay topic is often framed in terms of a research question, and the academic journal is the implied context for the essay. In terms of academia, the whole activity is authentic. There is also a welcome blurring of discipline boundaries in the proliferation of joint degrees. In this context, the idea that we should add a group project developing a literary guide to the Lake District for the Tourist Board may feel out of place, even though it may be closer to what many graduates end up doing. Although programmes in English literature may contain information about the publishing industry, marketing and the media, it appears more natural to hive off this sort of thing into a separate module on writing for a general audience or something similar. Indeed, one might say that I am arguing in this book that STEM subjects should learn from the humanities (apart from their unnecessary reliance on lectures) in terms of authenticity. And yet, where is the intrinsic feedback? Where is the experience of revision and resubmission? Does the student experience generally come close to the Oxbridge weekly one-to-one tutorial? The essay format cannot provide intrinsic feedback, but more group activity might, as would further explorations of interdisciplinary opportunities for the application of statistical analysis and serious games.

Sociology, economics and geography are disciplines with clear potential for a broader range of problem-based scenarios, and indeed one can find much on-line about project-based learning (although mainly at lower levels). In these areas, agent-based modelling (for example, [14–17]) and the availability of large data sets are offering opportunities for problem-based approaches. Whether a coherent degree programme in these disciplines (or some interdisciplinary combination) could be built round problem-based tuition is, I think, an interesting, open question.

5.5 Management

If a problem-based implementation is to be successful, it has to be wholehearted. By this I mean that reversion to the sage on the stage must be as close as possible to impossible. For example, there should simply not be enough contact time of the sort where instructors can revert to transmission of the whole content. Preparation for classes should feed very clearly into assessment, even if it is not directly assessed. In a flipped class, the sort of questions asked in the class must be related to the assessed exercises. The class should not just focus on conceptual muddles, while the assessed exercises remain only numerical substitutions or pattern-matching of equations. It is in essence a matter of the constructive alignment of the curriculum.

The main problem with implementation will be the response to issues that inevitably arise in the first run. These have to be seen as reasons for adopting the approach, not for abandoning it. I know of cases where student pressure has led to reversion to the lecture format, despite the fact that the problem-based approach gave better results. The problem-based cohort evidently believed their results would have been better had they been told more. They have no way of running the experiment for themselves to convince themselves otherwise.

Most management decisions come down to allocating resources: not just the workload on staff, but the student workload and the physical resources. There are two schools of thought here. On the one hand, in the first run, we start with a minimum, fit-for-purpose and add as little more as turns out to be necessary. This has the potential to derail the enterprise when, on the first presentation, fit-for-purpose turns out to be unfit-for purpose. The opposite approach of making sure that the first run is over-engineered with a view to reigning back later has the potential to alienate the exhausted participants.

An important issue is that of development costs. We tend to forget the cost of writing a lecture course, but are wary of start-up costs in problem-based approaches. It is probably true that the resource required to set up a problem-based pedagogy is greater than that for delivering a lecture course with problem sheets. The on-going resources can, however, be lower, depending on the class size. Small amounts of development funding can therefore provide longer term savings.

Facilitator training is another important issue. Some of the literature tends to imply that content knowledge is not essential for good facilitation. (For examples of contrary conclusions see [18] and [19].) Perhaps this depends on the context and the person. My personal experience is otherwise. I do not look back with satisfaction at the sessions I have tried to facilitate with limited content knowledge (and probably nor do the students). In theory, it is a defence against turning any student interaction into an excuse for a lecture, but that is best achieved by explaining the Socratic method to would-be facilitators. Let me take a simple example. Suppose that students are puzzled as to whether a hole in a flat metal plate expands or contracts as the plate is heated. I would ask them to consider the alternatives when the plate is cooled and see if that helps; and then perhaps provide a hint to look at the behaviour in a non-radial direction and see where their initial analysis had possibly led to the confusion. I do not think I could do that without some knowledge of physics.

Again referring to my personal experience, facilitator training seems to work best with an apprenticeship approach; initiates work alongside an experienced facilitator and their facilitation sessions are then observed. Training sessions involving fictitious scenarios or clips from actual sessions are often used, but our purely anecdotal experience is that they do not seem to work as effectively. One aspect on which we do have some albeit limited research data is the positive impact of specialist teaching instructors, who have ownership of the material, over facilitation by bought-in assistants, whether graduate students or academic staff [20, 21].

Problem-based tuition also requires institutional support: first and foremost physical space and time. Small scale problems can be worked through in small groups in a tiered lecture theatre, but the scope is limited if this is the only space available. When I started, the University had no large flat rooms with moveable furniture, because it was deemed an inefficient use of space. I booked a suite of classrooms and wedged the doors open to create an approximation to a common space for floating group facilitation. Nowadays, appropriate physical spaces are more common. The other main requirement is time: students cannot prepare for sessions if they have been given no time to do so. Classes have to be scheduled to support the learning not for administrative convenience. This becomes increasingly difficult as space allocation becomes centralized. But, then you have to ask, who is paying for this?

References

[1] PBL Clearinghouse (http://www1.udel.edu/inst/) (Accessed 20/9/2019)
[2] Raine D and Collett J 2003 Problem-based learning in astrophysics *Eur. J. Phys.* **24** S41
[3] Wikipedia 2019 (486958) 2014 MU_{69} (https://en.wikipedia.org/wiki/(486958)_2014_MU69) (Accessed 20/9/2019)
[4] NASA (http://Pluto.jhuapl.edu/Galleries/Featured-Images/picsMed/CA06_deconvolved.png?1554415198) (Accessed 20/9/2019)
[5] The Grenada Chocolate Company (https://www.grenadachocolate.com/tour/mix/) (Accessed 20/9/2019)
[6] Frank Leslie's Illustrated Newspaper 1858 (http://atlantic-cable.com/Article/1858Leslies/)
[7] Monro J 1981 *Heroes of the Telegraph* (London: The Religious Tract Society) (available at https://archive.org/details/heroestelegraph00munrgoog/page/n7 and in various republications)
[8] Morris M S and Thorne K S 1988 Wormholes in spacetime and their use for interstellar travel: a tool for teaching general relativity *Am. J. Phys.* **56** 395
[9] Gao J, Zhang W, Huang P, Zhang B, Zhang X and Xu B 2008 Intracellular spatial control of fluorescent magnetic nanoparticles *J. Am. Chem. Soc.* **130** 3710–1
[10] Thomas E and Raine D 2000 *Physics to a Degree* (London: Gordon and Breach)
[11] Fisher L 2002 *How to dunk a doughnut–the science of everyday life* (London: Weidenfeld & Nicolson)
[12] Clarke B L 1964 Multiple authorship trends in scientific papers *Science* **143** 822–4
[13] Vander Ven T M, Fisher B S, Cobane C T and Cullen F T 1998 How many authors does it take to publish an article? Trends and patterns in political science *Polit. Sci. Politics* **31** 847–56 (https://doi.org/10.2307/420730) Published online: 2 September 2013
[14] Epstein J M and Axtell R 1994 *Growing Artificial Societies* (Cambridge, MA: Brookings Institution Press & MIT Press)
[15] Paolucci M and Sacile R 2005 *Agent-Based Manufacturing and Control Systems* (Boca Raton, FL: CRC Press)
[16] Kimbrough S O 2012 *Agents, Games and Evolution: Strategies at Work and Play* (Boca Raton, FL: CRC Press)
[17] Squazzoni F 2012 *Agent-Based Computational Sociology* (New York: Wiley)
[18] Silver M and Wilkerson L 1991 Effects of tutors with subject expertise on the problem-based tutorial process *Acad. Med.* **66** 298–300
[19] Schmidt H G, Van der Arend A, Moust J H C, Kokx I and Boon L 1993 Influence of tutors' subject-matter expertise on student effort and achievement in problem-based learning *Acad. Med.* **68** 784–91
[20] Gretton S, Raine D and Bartle C 2014 Scaffolding problem based learning with module length problems *Conf.: European Science Education Research Association Conf. 2013* http://doi.org/10.13140/2.1.2156.4162
[21] Raine D 2013 Scaffolding problem-based learning *For the Love of Learning* ed T Bilham (Basingstoke: Palgrave) pp 84–8

IOP Publishing

Problem-Based Approaches to Physics
Changing perspectives in higher education
Derek Jeffrey Raine

Chapter 6

Do problem-based approaches work?

Let us start with some anecdotal reportage and then look at the research evidence for the effectiveness of problem-based approaches compared to more traditional methods centred around lectures. A problem-based approach is supposed to challenge students, take them out of their comfort zone, deepen their knowledge and develop their understanding. Of course, any state of confusion should be lifted by the end of the exercise, whenever that is. For many students, the realisation of the benefits of having been challenged happens fully only once they have entered the workplace.

Conversely, student dissatisfaction at the time is not evidence of getting the teaching right. Generally speaking, it is difficult to get it right on a first pass, because it is hard to predict the way students might respond to the structure of a problem-based implementation. As we have seen, a problem-based approach can be implemented in many different ways and with many different objectives. For example, the initial introduction of PBL in McMaster appears to have been motivated by the need to improve doctor-patient relations, not because students were failing to develop a satisfactory knowledge of anatomy. Evaluations which are based on changes in examination results (and hence on the acquisition of the type of knowledge that examinations test) may therefore give a skewed picture. One oft-repeated claim for PBL (and by implication for problem-based approaches in general) is that while there may be no increase in retention of information in the short term, much more is retained in the longer term than in traditional modes of learning. (See below.)

One other important point is that evaluations are often statistical; that is, we may prove that on average students learn better using a problem-based approach, but this may not be true of all students individually. In fact, at the very top of the spectrum of talent, it is most unlikely to be true, since traditional methods have produced generations of leading researchers and Nobel Prize winners. On the other hand, I doubt that in these cases a problem-based curriculum would do any harm.

At the opposite extreme, a well-designed problem-based approach, with its greater open-endedness and variety of assessments, has the potential to provide more opportunities for students to show what they can do, and not feel devalued for where they fail.

The meta-analyses we shall look at examine the impact of problem-based curricula on the student. In fact, it is also important to consider the impact on the teacher. Problem-based tuition allows for a much more detailed feedback from student to the instructor that can be used advantageously to adjust the pace and content of a curriculum. It is often claimed that PBL slows things down, permits less coverage and so on: what it actually does is to inform the instructor of realistic expectations as to what might be learnt by the student (as opposed to covered by the instructor) in a given time.

Turning then to the data, most studies use the term PBL to refer to the range of problem-based approaches, not just the McMaster model, so in this and the following sections, for consistency with the references, I will use the acronym PBL in this wider context. We can divide the outcomes of these studies into three groups which, in terms of the benefits of PBL over traditional approaches, we might label, yes, no and maybe.

Few studies enable direct comparison for reasons of either resources or ethics. Dividing a cohort into parallel PBL and non-PBL streams may be costly in staff time, and doing it compulsorily may be considered unethical. Some experiments with control groups have been carried out. No other has achieved quite the startling result reported from a physics course at DIT, where the PBL average class mark was 73%, while the other class scored in the low 40s [1]; however, the groups here were not randomly assigned, but chosen by the students. (See also [2, 3].) Examples of studies that find worthwhile effect sizes in comparable cohorts, where students have been randomly assigned between lecture-based and PBL classes for the same material, include [4] where it was found that PBL did not disadvantage students in terms of factual knowledge, while students found it more 'fun'. Cario *et al* [5] found a similar result in biology. This is a common outcome for PBL experienced as a single intervention and does not necessarily transfer to a whole programme. A similar result is found in [6] where student attitudes and teamwork skills very significantly improved in the PBL group. Dochy *et al* [7] examine 53 studies of PBL at the university level, only 4 of which report randomised control trials and 10 of which are elective, with much the same results: improvement in skills and little evidence of differences in knowledge on end-of-course tests. Comparisons between different year groups pre- and post- the transition to PBL are more common and potentially subject to both the novelty (or Hawthorne) effect and to publication bias. Dochy *et al* include four such trials, and many conference papers make similar comparisons between cohorts to support claims for the benefits of PBL.

Until recently, student views on PBL tended to be represented in the literature by what one might call happy quotes. For balance, it is interesting to note an ethnographic study [8] in which some medical students comment on how they felt that PBL was impacting negatively on their studies, while remembering that this is one cohort at one institution. A recent review of ethnographic studies in health sciences can be found in [9], representative of a growing interest in examining the process of learning in PBL rather than just measuring the outcomes.

Before we turn to the meta-studies, we need to distinguish between active learning and PBL. I will then summarise the results from a number of meta-analyses. Physics and physical sciences do not figure prominently in these studies with medicine and health care perhaps the largest areas. We shall then go on to look at the employers' viewpoint and the opinions of academic staff.

6.1 Results from active learning

'Why Minimal Guidance During Instruction Does Not Work: An Analysis of the Failure of Constructivist, Discovery, Problem-Based, Experiential, and Inquiry-Based Teaching' [10] is the title of a paper by Kirschner *et al* with a wide scope and pretty clear announcement of its results. It elicited a robust response [11] focussing on the claim that the very scope of the analysis undermined its conclusions:

> In this article, we first demonstrate that Kirschner *et al* have mistakenly conflated PBL and IL [inquiry learning] with discovery learning. We then present evidence demonstrating that PBL and IL are powerful and effective models of learning. Far from being contrary to many of the principles of guided learning that Kirschner *et al* discussed, both PBL and IL employ scaffolding extensively thereby reducing the cognitive load and allowing students to learn in complex domains. Moreover, these approaches to learning address important goals of education that include content knowledge, epistemic practices, and soft skills such as collaboration and self-directed learning.

Contrary to Kirschner *et al*, a number of meta-studies look at active learning more narrowly defined and find positive outcomes. Freeman *et al* [12] adopt the following definition:

> Active learning engages students in the process of learning through activities and/or discussion in class, as opposed to passively listening to an expert. It emphasizes higher-order thinking and often involves group work.

The most widely known analysis is that of Hake [13] who found that active learning produced learning gains in conceptual understanding in physics of almost two standard deviations above that of the traditional courses. (The learning gain is the (%mark post-test − %mark pre-test) divided by (100 − %mark pre-test); i.e. it is the fraction of the maximum possible increase actually achieved on average.) Freeman *et al* [12], in an analysis of 158 studies from the literature, find similarly that active learning in undergraduate STEM courses increases examination performance by around half a standard deviation. An analysis of 67 examples shows that it decreases failure rates from 34% to 22%. The authors comment on the failure rates thus:

the data suggest that 3,516 fewer students [out of 29 300] would have failed these STEM courses under active learning. [...] this translates into over US$3 500 000 in saved tuition dollars for the study population, had all students been exposed to active learning.

They add that had this been a randomised control experiment (which it was not) in medicine it might have been stopped because continuing to disadvantage the control group would have been unethical!

The case for the benefits of active learning therefore appears to be strong, but because the definition of active learning in [12] was so wide

...papers represent[ed] a wide array of active learning activities, including vaguely defined 'cooperative group activities in class,' in-class worksheets, clickers, problem-based learning (PBL), and studio classrooms, with intensities ranging from 10% to 100% of class time

we cannot use this result to draw conclusions about problem-based approaches in particular. In addition, the failure rates quoted are way beyond those that would be found in lecture-based courses in the UK, many of which include elements of active learning, so the benefits of a problem-based approach could arguably be less. So, let us turn to meta-analyses of more specifically problem-based pedagogies.

6.2 Meta-analyses of the impact of PBL

There is a large literature reporting on and analysing problem-based approaches across a wide range of institutions at both university and school or college level and in many countries, and numerous meta-analyses. The conclusions in this literature can, I think, be reduced to two aspects: the effect on the retention of knowledge and the impact on skills. (A possible third is on reducing drop-out rates.) To quote from [14]

With respect to students' retention of content, PBL research revealed an interesting tendency. In terms of short-term retention, either no difference was found between PBL and traditional students [15] or PBL students recalled slightly less [7]; yet, PBL students consistently outperformed traditional students on long-term retention assessments [16, 17].

While agreeing with the retention effect, Yew and Goh [18] note that none of the studies clarify what it is about problem-based pedagogy that leads to improved retention. Dochy *et al* [7] suggest that a possible explanation is the attention on elaboration in PBL [19]. This is clearly related to the point we made earlier on the way in which the pedagogy requires multiple modes of communication between students, and between students and instructors. Schmidt *et al* [20] argue that it is the combination of individual study and group activity that drives learning in PBL. The authors approach the issue through an analysis of the way in which PBL arouses interest, and the way in which discussion activates prior knowledge and leads to the retention of new knowledge. They also suggest an explanation for the lack of evidence of short-term learning gains from PBL through failure to control for differential drop-out rates. (These are lower in PBL programmes [21].)

The impact of problem-based pedagogy on the acquisition of skills is found universally, as might be expected. It is difficult to see how communication, group work or time management skills, to name a few, could be much improved by listening to a lecture course. Nevertheless, it is as well to have the evidence [22]:

> The results of these qualitatively synthesizing meta-analyses of PBL for preparation for the workplace indicate, however, that PBL is significantly more effective than traditional instruction to train competent and skilled practitioners and to promote long-term retention of knowledge and skills acquired during the learning experience or training session.

6.3 Employers' views on graduate employability

There is little if any direct evidence of the opinions of employers about problem-based pedagogy, but there is plenty of indirect evidence through the lens of employability. What we know from employers is the extent to which they value skills alongside content knowledge [23–25]. Required skills include [26] skills in communication, computation, technological literacy, and information retrieval, the ability to arrive at informed judgments (by effectively defining problems, gathering and evaluating information), the ability to function in a global community, adaptability, ease with diversity, motivation and persistence, ethical and civil behaviour, creativity and resourcefulness, technical competence, and the ability to work with others, AND (as if the list were not already long enough) a demonstrated ability to deploy all of the previous characteristics to develop workable solutions in complex, real-world settings.

The important point about this list is not that it is unachievable, but that it is not about what the individual teacher can do; it is about curriculum design. There is some evidence in engineering (presumably led by employers) that accrediting bodies are starting to call for problem-based curricula [27].

One area where the longer term impact of PBL on workplace performance has been studied is in medical education. The outcomes here seem mixed. A questionnaire to medical educators produced a range of opinions on the efficacy of PBL in comparison to traditional teaching [28]. More nuanced research studies claim generally positive outcomes [29]. Neville [30] finds that, despite the methodological difficulties of heterogeneous samples, there is evidence that 'graduates of PBL curricula demonstrate equivalent or superior professional competencies compared with graduates of more traditional curricula'. On the other hand, numerous reviews reach the opposite conclusion. For example, [31]: 'There is no evidence from this study that PBL graduates are better able to maintain competence than graduates of conventional schools'. Or [32]: 'The review of the literature revealed no convincing evidence that PBL improves knowledge base and clinical performance, at least not of the magnitude that would be expected given the resources required for a PBL curriculum'.

Most of these comparisons appear to be between the traditional lecture-based curriculum and the medical model of PBL. There is some evidence that students prefer what is perceived to be the more focussed pedagogy of case-based learning [33, 34]. However, as we have mentioned previously, student preferences are not necessarily a good guide to effective learning, so more extensive follow-up studies are needed. In any case, the general confounding factor here is the very high quality of medical students: we might expect them to succeed pretty well in any curriculum. Comparable studies in engineering and professions such as business and management, which have a wider range of entry qualifications (in the UK at least) would be of interest.

An important aspect of employability is the students' ability, or lack of ability, to articulate the skills they acquire. Surveys of (a relatively small number of) students in Natural Science programmes taught by problem-based tuition [35, 36] show evidence of growing confidence in skills attributes across the programme, but it is when we come to talk to graduates in employment that we see the strongest realisation of the impact of problem-based tuition. To a large extent, such surveys can be dismissed as expeditions fishing for compliments from the self-selected cohorts that respond. More research is needed to determine what works in higher education from the perspective of graduates in employment and employers rather than from current students.

6.4 Buy-in from staff and senior management

When I proposed introducing PBL group projects into our laboratory, as part of the options packages for the different degree streams (in Physics, Astrophysics, Space Science and Technology), one member of staff spent a long afternoon telling me why it would not work. The following day, to my surprise, he came to my office to say that he had thought about it, and that perhaps it would work. At the end of the module, he again came to my office to tell me that 'I had changed his life'. For the first time in his career, he had actually enjoyed his time in the laboratory with the students.

Gratifying as this is, it is an outlier. My experience more generally has been pressure from colleagues to 'tell students what they need to know', in other words, to creep back to the transmissive approach to learning. Students are not immune from this pressure either. One year a group of our students got up a petition to call for PBL to be abolished. Interestingly, another group of students in that year came and told me not to worry about the petition: they assured me that they understood what we were trying to do. In Natural Sciences, where we taught the whole programme by problem-based tuition, we were fortunate to start with a very small group. This makes it relatively easy to implement mid-course corrections in response to student feedback.

One might wonder why piloting a module of problem-based tuition does not iron out all of the problems. The answer is that students view a single module quite differently from a more extensive programme. On the one hand, students tend to appreciate the change, and the emphasis on skills, and look at it as a de-emphasis on content (for example, [37]). On the other hand, a single problem-based module can be an unwelcome disruption to an established pattern of study, particularly if it is a high-stakes activity. In some cases, staff have had to abandon a problem-based approach under pressure from students or senior management.

We have already discussed staff resistance on the basis of particular content. This may be an excuse, or it may be justified. Often there is a potential barrier that can be overcome, as we saw above for technically complex or advanced subjects. I have taught both relativity and quantum theory through problem-based tuition, and it was greatly rewarding. I have never taught a problem-based cosmology course, and I am not sure I would want to (although others might), but I have used flipped learning to teach cosmology (before the term was invented). The difference is that cosmology is not applied to anything—it is an end in itself (cosmologists do not solve problems other than their own) whereas quantum theory can be applied (e.g. to quantum dots) and relativity can be applied (to GPS or, more speculatively, to construct a time machine). We have also noted the gradation between problems and projects, and the multiple ways of implementing and scaffolding problem-based approaches. My point here is that buying-in should not mean selling-out, that is ceding ownership. (See also section 4.8.)

Staff antipathetic to PBL invariably raise issues of content coverage and resources: my course is too basic/too advanced, my class is too large/too small, I/my students would not be comfortable with this approach, my colleagues/ head of department/ senior management would not approve (delete according to audience). Table 6.1 gives the results of a survey of academic staff attitudes to PBL in one institution, which is nevertheless probably representative.

6.5 Problem-based approaches across cultures

In [38], we find contributions on PBL from Finland, Malaysia, Abu Dhabi, the USA, Thailand, the UK, Denmark, Japan, Australia, Spain, Ireland, Bahrain, Korea, New Zealand, Singapore and the Netherlands. PBL is also widely adopted in South America and practiced in India and Pakistan. Much of the activity is at school level (K-12), but many countries have individual PBL enthusiasts or government-supported programmes [39]. Note though that some programmes use the acronym PBL to refer to project-based learning.

More widely, the PAN-PBL organisation [40] grew from the Pan American Network in 2000 to a world-wide professional association (although membership is pre-dominantly North and South American and European) with biennial conferences.

The Aalto Global Impact (AGI) project [41] is a recent project which aims to promote problem-based learning in South Asia. It has received €1 million funding from the European Commission through the Erasmus programme. The countries involved are India, Nepal, Bhutan, in collaboration with institutions in Finland, the Netherlands and Lithuania. The Citylab project, also part-funded by the EU, seeks

Table 6.1. Outcome space that describes the different ways lecturers perceive of PBL. Reproduced with permission from [38], Aalborg Universitet.

Category	Perception
Positive	It is a student-centred approach that supports the development of conceptual understanding, problem-solving skills and other key skills
	It models the learning that occurs in the research process and it is therefore more effective than passive learning
Negative	It is not a suitable approach for the physical sciences, as they are conceptual subjects that cannot be taught through this approach
	It slows the learning process and therefore it is not possible to cover the required and necessary content
	It is only suitable for developing problem-solving skills with students who already have the required knowledge
	It concentrates more on the development of skills that are not necessary to be a physicist
	It requires far too many resources and too much effort on the part of the lecturers
	It is just the current fad and will not last
Neutral	It is a better approach than the traditional approach but it requires extra resources and effort
	It predominantly works because of the social dimension but it would be less resource intensive to simply introduce more group activities
	It requires far too much work and resources and therefore its use will fade out

to develop a PBL approach to enhance higher education in South America through PBL [42].

In [43], 13 controlled studies in China show higher gains in knowledge and skills of the PBL cohorts. Perhaps more interesting than these gains is the knowledge that PBL has gained more than a foothold in Chinese medical education. Some researchers note the existence of cultural barriers. An investigation of PBL in Asian universities [44] found that a key impediment to engagement with PBL was the cultural inappropriateness of challenging peers or the tutor. In [45], these difficulties are put down to personality types (based on the Myers–Briggs Type Indicator (MBTI)) which indicate greater introversion amongst the Chinese compared to English applicants. They claim that introverts are less likely to express an opinion. We found the issue of questioning supposed authority to be a barrier to engagement in a workshop in Singapore, although a reluctance of strangers to talk to each other in these cultures may also have played a part. Given the enthusiastic embrace of PBL in Singapore Polytechnic, such barriers cannot be insurmountable, or even particularly difficult to break down, here and probably elsewhere.

6.6 The future of problem-based pedagogies

Are problem-based approaches just a fad (with a long half-life), or the gateway to a 21st-century curriculum? Fads or fashions die when they fail to live up to expectations or something better, or more entertaining, comes along. We have certainly experienced that in education.

New pedagogies come and go; lectures are with us forever, or at least since the Atheneum. One of the great mysteries of education is how lecture-based pedagogy survived the printing press. It can have nothing to do with learning per se. It seems to have more to do with creating a community. For this reason, a reliance on lectures will survive the digital revolution if we let it. This would be a missed opportunity.

That is not to say a sense of community is not important. As we saw, evidence from the UK National Student Survey (NSS) and the Student Engagement Survey (UKSES), as well as from our own research, points to the opposite. However, while the mere act of worship (attending the lectures and taking notes) on its own may help create a sense of belonging, even where much of the liturgy is in an arcane language, this is not a strong community tie (and can be alienating for, for example, minority groups). Problem-based approaches that involve, in particular, small-stakes group activity are likely to be more effective (and certainly not less so).

Nevertheless, the pressures in higher education point in the opposite direction. Large lecture groups are efficient in delivering contact hours (in a meaningless way, of course) and in providing more contact hours as evidence (misplaced, of course) of value for money. Fewer assessments reduce the marking load on staff and the stress on students (and reduce the opportunities for feedback, i.e. learning). Less stress (effort?) translates to better NSS scores, more students and more income to support research.

It does not have to be like this. We shall see in the final chapter how problem-based pedagogies in a developing context could change the way we deliver higher education to the benefit of students, of research, of the economy and of society.

References

[1] Bowe B and Cowan J 2004 A comparative evaluation of problem-based learning in physics: a lecture-based course and a problem-based course *Challenging Research into Problem-Based Learning* ed M Savin-Baden and K Wilkie (SRHE/Open University Press) (see also https://www.irishtimes.com/news/education/dit-s-novel-problem-solving-approach-to-physics-is-great-fun-say-students-1.1086138)

[2] Bowe B W, Daly S, Flynn C and Howard R 2003 Problem-based learning: an approach to enhancing learning and understanding of optics for first-year students *Proc. SPIE 4876, Opto-Ireland 2002: Optics and Photonics Technologies and Applications* https://doi.org/10.1117/12.463956

[3] Celik P, Onder F and Silay I 2011 The effects of problem-based learning on the students' success in physics course *Proc. Social Behav. Sci.* **28** 656–60 (World Conf. on Educational Technology Researches–2011)

[4] Antepohl W and Herzig S 1999 Problem-based learning versus lecture-based learning in a course of basic pharmacology: a controlled, randomized study *Med. Educ.* **33** 106–13

[5] Carrió M, Larramona P, Baños J E and Pérez J 2011 The effectiveness of the hybrid problem-based learning approach in the teaching of biology: a comparison with lecture-based learning *J. Biol. Educ.* **45** 229–35

[6] Mantri A, Dutt S, Gupta J P and Chitkara M 2008 Design and evaluation of a PBL-based course in analog electronics *IEEE Trans. Educ.* **51** 432–8

[7] Dochy F, Segers M, den Bossche P V and Gijbels D 2003 Effects of problem-based learning: a meta-analysis *Learning and Instruction* **13** 533–68

[8] Ann Bunting M 2016 Medical education & problem-based learning: collaboration, contradiction & conflict *PhD thesis* University of East Anglia (https://ueaeprints.uea.ac.uk/59464/1/Bunting_Thesis_2016.pdf)

[9] Jin J and Bridges S 2016 Qualitative research in pbl in health sciences education: a review *Interdiscip. J. Problem-Based Learn.* **10** https://doi.org/10.7771/1541-5015.1605

[10] Kirschner P A, Sweller J and Clark R E 2006 Why minimal guidance during instruction does not work: an analysis of the failure of constructivist, discovery, problem-based, experiential, and inquiry-based teaching *Educat. Psychol.* **41** 75–86

[11] Hmelo-Silver C E, Duncan R G and Chinn C A 2006 Scaffolding and achievement in problem-based and inquiry learning: a response to Kirschner, Sweller, and Clark *Educat. Psychol.* **42** 99–107

[12] Freeman S *et al* 2014 Active learning increases student performance in science, engineering, and mathematics *Proc. Natl. Acad. Sci.* **111** 8410–15

[13] Hake R 1998 Interactive-engagement vs traditional methods: a six- thousand-student survey of mechanics test data for introductory physics courses *Am. J. Phys.* **66** 64–74

[14] Hung W, Jonassen D H and Liu R 2007 Problem-based learning *Handbook of Research on Educational Communications and Technology* ed J Michael Spector, M David Merrill, J van Merriënboer and M P Driscoll (Abingdon: Routledge) (https://doi.org/10.4324/9780203880869)

[15] Gallagher S A and Stepien W J 1996 Content acquisition in problem-based learning: depth versus breadth in American studies *J. Educ. Gifted* **19** 257–75

[16] Mårtenson D, Eriksson H and Ingelman-Sundberg M 1985 Medical chemistry: evaluation of active and problem-oriented teaching methods *Med. Educ.* **19** 34–42

[17] Norman G R and Schmidt H G 1992 The psychological basis of problem-based learning: a review of the evidence *Acad. Med.* **67** 557–65 (Norman and Schmidt cite Tans R W *et al* 1986 Tijdschrift voor Onderwijsresearch 35–46, in Dutch)

[18] Yew E H J and Goh K 2016 Problem-based learning: an overview of its process and impact on learning *Health Profess. Educ.* **2** 75–9

[19] Schmidt H G 1990 Innovative and conventional curricula compared: what can be said about their effects? *Innovation in Medical Education: An Evaluation of Its Present Status* ed Z H Nooman, H G Schmidt and E S Ezzat (New York: Springer) pp 1–7

[20] Schmidt H G, Rotgans J and Yew E H J 2011 The process of problem-based learning: what works and why *Med. Educ.* **45** 792–806

[21] Schmidt H G, Cohen-Schotanus J and Arends L R 2009 Impact of problem-based, active learning on graduation rates for 10 generations of dutch medical students *Med. Educ.* **43** 211–8

[22] Strobel J and van Barneveld A 2009 When is pbl more effective? A meta-synthesis of meta-analyses comparing pbl to conventional classrooms *Interdiscip. J. Problem-Based Learn.* **3**

[23] Wingspread Conference 1994 *Quality Assurance in Undergraduate Education: What the Public Expects* (Denver, CO: Education Commission of the States) (https://www.aspa-usa.org/wp-content/uploads/2015/03/Quality-Assurance-in-Undergraduate-Education-What-the-Public-Expects-June-1994.pdf)

[24] Hanson S and Overton T 2010 *Skills required by chemistry graduates and their development in degree programmes* (York: Higher Education Academy)

[25] Hill M A, Overton T L, Thompson C D, Kitson R R A and Coppo P 2019 Undergraduate recognition of curriculum-related skill development and the skills employers are seeking *Chem. Educ. Res. Pract.* **20** 68–84

[26] Savery J R 2006 Overview of problem-based learning: definitions and distinctions *Interdiscip. J. Problem-Based Learn.* 1 https://doi.org/10.7771/1541-5015.1002

[27] Wallace M F G and Webb A W 2016 In the midst of a shift: undergraduate stem education and pbl enactment **46** 47–55 (available at: http://search.ebscohost.com.ezproxy3.lib.le.ac.uk/login.aspx?direct=true&db=eric&AN=EJ1119858&site=ehost-live)

[28] Tavakol M, Dennick R and Tavakol S 2009 A descriptive study of medical educators' views of problem-based learning *BMC Med. Educ.* **9** 2009

[29] Schmidt H G, van der Molen H T, Te Winkel W W R and Wijnen W H F 2009 Constructivist, problem-based learning does work: a meta-analysis of curricular comparisons involving a single medical school *Educ. Psychol.* **44** 227–49

[30] Neville A J 2009 Problem-based learning and medical education forty years on: a review of its effects on knowledge and clinical performance *Med. Princ. Pract.* **18** 1–9

[31] Norman G R, Wenghofer E and Klass D 2008 Predicting doctor performance outcomes of curriculum interventions: problem-based learning and continuing competence *Med. Educ.* **42** 794

[32] Colliver J A 2000 Effectiveness of problem-based learning curricula: research and theory *Acad. Med.* **75** 259–66

[33] McLean S F 2016 Case-based learning and its application in medical and health-care fields: a review of worldwide literature *J. Med. Educ. Circ. Dev.* **3** https://doi.org/10.4137/JMECD.S20377

[34] Srinivasan M, Wilkes M, Stevenson F, Nguyen T and Slavin S 2007 Comparing problem-based learning with case-based learning: effects of a major curricular shift at two institutions *Acad. Med.* **82** 74–82

[35] Symons S L, Andrew C and Harvey Chad T 2017 Student perceptions of staged transfer to independent research skills during a four-year honours science undergraduate program *Can. J. Scholar. Teach. Learn.* **8** 6

[36] Gretton S and Raine D Development of employability skills in problem-based tuition (unpublished)

[37] Williams D P 2015 Problem based learning approaches to teaching chemistry *Inquiry-Based Learning for Science, Technology, Engineering, and Math (STEM) Programs: A Conceptual and Practical Resource for Educators (Innovations in Higher Education Teaching and Learning)* vol 4 ed P Blessinger and J M Carfora (Emerald Group Publishing Limited) pp 93–112 https://doi.org/10.1108/S2055-364120150000004007

[38] Bowe B 2013 The relationship between conceptions of teaching and learning and perceptions of problem-based learning among physics faculty *PBL Across Cultures, The 4th Int. Research Symp. on Problem-Based Learning (IRSPBL)* ed K Mohd-Yusof, M Arsat, M T Borhan, E de Graaff, A Kolmos and F A Phang (Aalborg: Aalborg University Press) pp 364–72 (https://vbn.aau.dk/ws/portalfiles/portal/80390072/PBL_across_Cultures.pdf)

[39] Hmelo-Silver C E 2012 Int. perspectives on problem-based learning: Contects, cultures, challenges and adaptations *Interdiscipl. J. Problem-Based Learn.* **6** https://doi.org/10.7771/1541-5015.1310

[40] PAN-PBL: Association of Problem-Based Learning and Active Learning Methodologies (http://www.panpbl.org/about/)
[41] See Aalto University 2018 New cooperative project develops problem-based learning in South Asia (https://www.aalto.fi/en/news/new-cooperative-project-develops-problem-based-learning-in-south-asia)
[42] Citylab LA (https://www.uantwerpen.be/en/projects/citylab-la--engaging/citylab-project/)
[43] Wang J, Xu Y, Liu X, Xiong W, Xie J and Zhao J 2016 Assessing the effectiveness of problem-based learning in physical diagnostics education in China: a meta-analysis *Sci. Rep.* **6** 36279
[44] Raja Hussaina R M, Wan Mamata W H, Salleha N, Saata R M and Harland R 2007 Problem-based learning in Asian universities *Stu. Higher Educ.* **32** 761–72
[45] Huang B, Zheng L, Li C, Li L and Yu H 2013 Effectiveness of problem-based learning in chinese dental education: a meta-analysis *J. Dent. Educ.* **77** 377–83

Chapter 7

Problem-based approaches: looking to the future

7.1 Structural change: the teaching focussed lecturer

The development of the university is like that of most institutions, an essay in evolving complexity. The original purpose was the apparently straightforward mission to teach what was known. In law and geometry, this might simply involve teaching from the book. As early as the 13th century, however, teaching philosophy from the book—in this case Aristotle—came into conflict with teaching from the other book (the Christian Bible). The revelation of troublesome concepts led to research—the seeking after truth—although this was conducted largely outside the universities, supported by patronage, right up until the 19th century. The research-led university was first established in Germany by Wilhelm Humboldt and copied in the establishment of universities in the United States. We looked at the subsequent developments in the UK in chapter 1.

More recently we have seen a fracturing and complexity of roles as shown in figures 7.1 and 7.2. The simple division between teaching and research activities (or between research, teaching and service) no longer adequately captures the role of the university academic. Traditionally (which in the UK means dating from the expansion of the university sector in the 1950s), early-career academics would generally be appointed for their research, with less emphasis on their role as teachers. As their careers progressed they might be expected to bear more of the burden of administration, and their role might evolve to focus more on teaching. This simple picture has been complicated by the additional roles that academics are now expected to fulfill. These include demonstrating the relevance and impact of their research through links with external bodies and the media ('third stream'), outreach activities (aka marketing) to promote their institution to potential students, and a larger teaching and administrative load that accompanies declining staff–student ratios. Concurrently, pressure for change has come from the Research Excellence Framework (REF) in the UK, which periodically produces league tables of research activity and impact, with implications for research funding. Under these pressures,

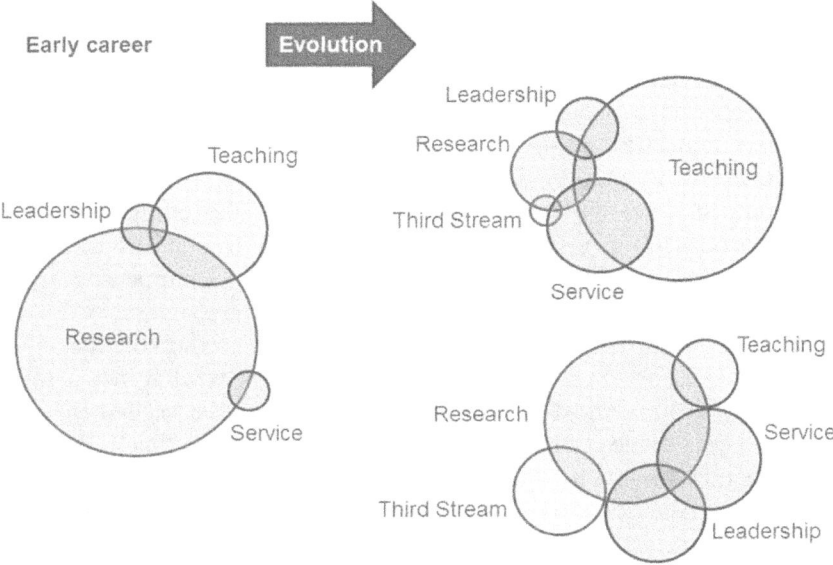

Figure 7.1. The traditional career progression in academia.

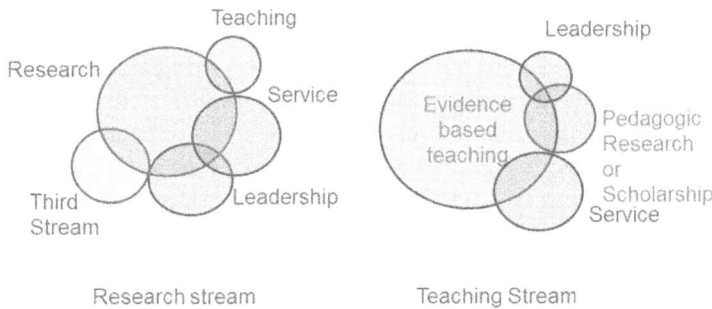

Figure 7.2. The evolving career progression in academia.

the role of the teaching-focussed lecturer (or teaching fellow) has emerged (figure 7.2) with a prime responsibility for teaching and thereby excluded from the REF metrics.

As I have indicated in figure 7.2 by labelling teaching as evidence based, the division of labour consequent on the appointment of academic staff with a prime responsibility for teaching rather than research has the potential to change the environment for pedagogic innovation. We saw in chapter 5 some evidence of how a dedicated teaching team can improve learning outcomes. The threat to this virtuous circle is the tactical approach to the REF, whereby less productive researchers are re-assigned to teaching-focussed roles for which they have limited enthusiasm.

This division of labour, properly managed, offers advantages for both teaching and research. For teaching, dedicated staff have time to take on board the pedagogy they learn in programmes of staff development, and use it to inform practice. They have time to disseminate their practice and inform others. In short, they have time to take a scholarly approach to university education as professional teachers. Researchers, on the other hand, are then freed from the burden of routine delivery and assessment of basic content and can contribute supervision of undergraduate projects and occasional inspirational lectures related to their research. The division of labour, executed strategically in this way, would improve both teaching and research. However, to qualify as a strategy for enhancing education, teaching-focussed staff must have ownership of the programme as a teaching team, and not be isolated individuals filling in the gaps. The danger is that the division of labour promotes a drift toward the casualisation of teaching as is happening in the USA and Australia [1, 2].

One aspect that can be addressed with this strategy is the so-called burden of assessment. Assessment—meaning meaningful feedback—is what instructors should be spending much if not most of their time doing. We have argued that problem-based approaches provide contexts for meaningful intrinsic feedback. But, this needs to be supplemented as much as possible by extrinsic feedback in conditions where that feedback can be used, which, as we saw, implies further assessment of the same material. This is almost impossible to provide in a research-intensive institution without at least de facto teaching teams.

Furthermore, teaching teams offer the opportunity to take control of the curriculum and design it as a whole. Traditionally, the design of a physics curriculum consists largely in putting electromagnetism 2 after electromagnetism 1, adding some skills based activity somewhere and putting a project at the end. On the contrary, as we have argued, the design of the whole needs to be considered in terms of the student journey. Individual modules need to balance core learning of definitions and relations, with conceptual understanding and problem solving, alongside the development of transferable skills through appropriate design. What is the appropriate design? That is the point: it is intervention, evaluation, reflection and iteration. Instructors learn from the feedback they get from the 'real world' (i.e. doing not just thinking). The Kolb cycle [3] (chapter 2) applies to educational practice as much as it does to student learning.

This emerging structure also offers further opportunities for an evidence-based approach to learning in higher education. Particularly in STEM subjects, there have been many small scale, local initiatives, but little on a national level. Larger scale programmes have largely been funded as time-limited projects, even where recipients signed up to continuation strategies. (For example the CETLs; see chapter 1.) But, educational impact requires long time-scales and evidence requires large scale longitudinal studies. This becomes possible once there is a cohort of dedicated teachers in higher education. At present, pedagogic research in higher education is a Cinderella subject in the UK, largely unfunded in small outcrops. But, the increase in access to higher education cannot be accomplished by a simple scaling up of the traditional approach; there have been great changes in the environment of higher education. We need to understand the impact of these changes and how best to accommodate them. There are a multitude of innovations happening at the course or module level some of which will turn out to be seminal. There is less innovation at a strategic or programme level. In particular, changes in technology have generated new modes of interaction with students and between students. We need research to understand how best to use these, particularly how staff and students react to these various media.

We know from the early attempts to put students in front of computer simulations that the computer-human interaction is a crucial part of the simulation design. There is a vast potential for teaching physics by immersing students in virtual worlds. It is unlikely that education will ever have the resources to build its own dedicated infrastructure, so we need to know how to take advantage of what exists (or will exist). I do not think this can happen unless dedicated teaching teams have the resources to collaborate on a national scale.

A final relatively unexplored territory is the use of simulations to model the process of education, particularly agent-based modelling, in order to unravel the complexity of educational interactions. This would enable us to test our understanding of qualitative models of ways of promoting learning [4–6]. Of course, such models will be highly simplified, at least initially, but how can we be sure of our conceptualisation of the complex process of learning unless we can understand simple models?

I have argued in this section that we need to look in more depth and more strategically at structural changes in higher education. In the next section, I will return to broader reasons why we need to rethink pedagogies.

7.2 Physics and society

The importance of higher education for the economy, in the sciences in particular, has been well rehearsed. I will come back to the importance of other disciplines in section 7.6. If we need more scientists, we have to recruit them from the existing pool of young people. If there is anything we have learnt from the last 30 years, it is that our current marketing strategy has not been an outstanding success. (If it had we would not still be discussing this.) Because the recruitment process starts at school, it can be successful only if we have a supportive school curriculum and well-qualified teachers. Where do the teachers come from? From the universities. Where does the curriculum come from? From the universities. So, we have to ask whether the university curriculum is fit for purpose. In particular, does it provide the environment for changes to the school curriculum that would encourage recruitment to science? We have to look at the supply side as well as the demand side. What is the product?

School science is not normally taught by lectures and problem sheets (although I know of teachers who adopted this pedagogy 50 years ago). And a few brave souls use PBL in schools with classes where there is little danger of pupils not getting A^*s, however they are taught. It is unlikely therefore that we can attribute the lack of interest in science to the way the subject is taught. It may be that inspiring teachers can do a brilliant job with any material, but it would be better if the product could be delivered by the merely competent. We need to examine whether the problem is not just the lack of specialist teachers (although this surely contributes), but if there is an issue with what is taught. It is well known that children tend to lose their natural inquisitiveness around age fourteen, and develop an idea of what does and does not interest them. It has to be admitted that Newton's laws do not figure often enough on the interesting side of the divide. Adolescents generally have more pressing issues.

Universities must therefore produce graduate teachers who are willing to rethink curricula in order to generate engagement through what is taught, not just how it is taught. I will come back to a suggestion in the next section. First I want to look at how this fits a bigger picture of university education.

The existence of a technically qualified workforce is both a public and private benefit. This is so obvious that it needs no emphasis; without an industrial surplus, there would be no universities. However, whether institutions of higher education dedicated solely to the production of an industrial surplus would deserve to be called universities is another matter. Somehow we need to capture the importance of knowledge for its own sake, without the absurdity of implying an equality of value for all knowledge. On the contrary, a university education should instil a discriminatory sense of what is valuable and what is not. We may not agree completely on our choices, but we need to be able to articulate a defence of our values. This leads us to a rather different view of the purpose of a university education in general, and one for physics in particular, from the vocational model.

At the extremes, a university education is held to be a purely public benefit or alternatively a purely selfish experience. Perhaps the truth lies somewhere in between. But, what sort of public benefit and where do the individual benefits lie? An educated population is rightly held to be a foundation for democracy. In a modern society, it is impossible for an individual, however, educated, to have the necessary expertise needed to make an informed decision on more than a relatively narrow specialism. But, a university graduate should perhaps be able to distinguish between informed and uninformed opinion (or fake news). Access to information has become increasingly democratised, first through the printing press and now through electronic media. Learning how to avail oneself of these resources—learning how to study—is a by-product (hopefully) of a university education. Perhaps it ought to be more emphasised explicitly at the school level.

Universities provide, or ought to provide in a functioning democracy, social mobility. We have in the UK a range of higher education institutions with a range of programmes which serve a diverse set of students. Good universities serve well the students they admit; a reputation for research is not essential. Social mobility means admitting those students with the talent (and desire) to succeed, which means in turn finding and nurturing talent in schools. This is particularly problematic in physics where the 7% (15% over age 16) of pupils in private education (i.e. public schools in the UK) are taught by a disproportionate fraction of physics specialist teachers and provide 20% of the university cohort.

We therefore have two basic reasons for rethinking pedagogy in higher education: the economic role and the social role. In the next section, I will examine what this might mean for physics education. I leave other disciplines to experts in those disciplines. My argument here is that the design of the curriculum has an important role to play in schools, just as it does in universities. The two are linked because the school teacher of tomorrow is the university undergraduate of today.

Table 7.1. Physics as history: the main topics, the century in which the modern study began and some landmark dates.

Century	Topic	Landmarks
C17	Mechanics,	Newton (1687), Laplace (1799)
	Geometrical optics	Snell's Law (1621), Huygens (1690)
C18	Electricity	Coulomb (1784), Volta (1800)
C19	Physical optics,	Young (1803), Fresnel (1818)
	Electromagnetism,	Oersted (1819), Faraday (1831), Maxwell (1873), Hertz (1887)
	Statistical physics	Boltzmann (1875), Gibbs (1876)
C20	Relativity,	Einstein (1905)
	Quantum physics,	Heisenberg, Schrodinger (1926)
	Condensed matter physics	Drude (1900), Debye (1912), Bragg (1913), Sommerfeld (1928), Bloch (1928), Brillouin (1930)

7.3 What is physics?

We have argued the need to re-evaluate how physics should be presented. So, let us start with some attempts to define the subject matter.

- Physics is the science of matter and energy and their interactions [7].
- Physics (from the Greek, φυσικoζ (phusikos), 'natural', and φυσιζ (phusis), 'nature') is the science of Nature in the broadest sense [8].
- Physics is about asking fundamental questions (such as what are the basic building blocks of matter) and trying to answer them by observing and experimenting [9].

I do not feel that these are very successful at capturing what the subject is about (unless you already know) or generating enthusiasm (but it might be a bit demanding to generate enthusiasm for a definition). Rather than trying to define the container, an alternative is to specify the contents. Table 7.1 is how physics appears as a list of topics. The problem is that it looks like a history lesson; even the 20th century is the distant past for the contemporary school pupil. It is as if we were presented with a dinner menu that listed the contents in terms of the percentages of fats, sugars, proteins and so on. It is what is done with these ingredients that makes the meal appealing.

I do not have any issue with a university curriculum conceived in this way (largely because I know it will end up very much in the 21st century) although as the reader will perhaps be aware, I think it should be taught by a problem-based approach. My concern is that this is the curriculum, in simplified form, that is handed down to schools (although I note that the Scottish government have tried to reform this and the Welsh government are in the process of so doing).

There are many ways we might distill the essence of physics; figure 7.3 outlines one.

Measurement	Use of Analogies
Averages	Mathematical models
Rates of change	Change of frames of reference
Orders of magnitude	Symmetry
Estimates	Conservation laws, (energy, momentum)
Proportionality	Open and closed systems
Intensive and extensive variables	Equilibrium, dynamic equilibrium
Graphical analysis	Irreversibility
Derivation of hypothesis from experiment	Description of bulk properties in terms of constituents
Use of a physical law for prediction	Fluctuations
	Transport
Discrediting of a hypothesis by experiment	Wave concepts
	Resonance
Classic experiments overturning prior beliefs	Frequency space
	Phase space
Phenomenological laws	Concept of a field
Physical Reductionism	Quantum properties

Figure 7.3. Concepts of physics.

How does this help? As it stands, it is not necessarily more exciting than any of the previous characterisations. But, I think that many of these concepts can be illustrated in many ways that are not necessarily connected with physics. We can then show how, applied to examples from the physical world, these concepts take on precise meanings and allow us to understand and solve a range of simple problems. In this way, we have a hope of starting from a point of interest expressed in language that is meaningful, and moving on to see how physics uses these ideas with greater precision. If we can invent an example where it is possible to see that knowing physics makes a difference, so much the better.

Take an example: the lever (which comes under several of the heading in figure 7.3). Why do we think that mechanical advantage and velocity ratios are of any interest to the typical early teen? The answer is that they are a simple way to understand the manner in which the material world around us was created through technology: exchange the impossible (a large force for a short time) for the possible (a small force for a long time). Furthermore, the exchange can be calculated by our typical early teen. Students do not need to know this on the grounds that it will be directly useful in using a jack to change a car wheel (or anything else), because it will not. They just follow the instructions in the manual (rather as they will have learnt to do in calculating the mechanical advantage). The real point is more subtle. I do not believe that many teens are impressed by great scientific and technical achievements; such things are just there. Knowing how a transistor works does not make the music any sweeter. But, if they can appreciate how a lever works, and how the associated trade-off underpins the industrial revolution, then they are on the way to becoming a scientist. Will a lecture on the lever achieve this? I doubt that levers are taught by lectures in many or any schools. The subject is ripe for a problem-based approach: not just because the law of the lever is on the syllabus, but because it is the basis of that larger generalization. This might open the door to discussions of leverage and trade-offs in other contexts, biological and social. So, we start with the idea of leverage, we make it precise in the context of physics and then we return to discuss the concept in general.

How might we illustrate that knowing about the lever could make a difference. Suppose we return to the origin of the lever in Ancient Egypt, where it was used to draw water from the Nile (as well as moving stone slabs). We might ask whether it is quicker to raise water using a long lever and a large (heavy) bucket a few times or a shorter lever and a lighter bucket many times. (With a frictionless machine and massless buckets one might guess that it should not make any difference, because the work done in both cases is the same. But, the performing of an experiment might lead to an interesting discussion.)

Thinking of problems like this (or better) is hard. But, it is easier if we do not operate in discipline silos, something we turn to next.

7.4 Interdisciplinarity

Most socially relevant problems are interdisciplinary. As an article in the *New Scientist* put it [10]: Forget biology, chemistry or physics—the most exciting research is happening at the interface of the disciplines.

It is a widely held opinion that pupils have to be clear about discipline distinctions and hence what physics is, lest they are confused when it comes to making choices (about three A-level subjects, at age 16 in the UK). I think this is a red herring. I do not see pupils being confused as to the distinction between history, geography and english when they are taught as humanities. There is a pretty clear distinction between what happens in a chemistry, biology and physics laboratory. The retreat from discipline silos broadens the perceived relevance of physics. Indeed some optional modules at A-level verge on the interdisciplinary (presumably because physics actually is relevant).

To return to the example of the lever and the principle of amplification: this is ubiquitous in biology. Perhaps the most immediately engaging application would be to epidemics. And then we might understand autocatalytic reactions and explosions (always popular) and hence some chemistry. My point is not to propose this as specific content for a new curriculum, but to illustrate the way in which an interdisciplinary curriculum opens up all sorts of possibilities for developing students' interest in science in general, and in physics in particular.

Of course, this is more easily implemented if teachers themselves have a working knowledge across the disciplines. For science teachers, I would advocate that they study natural sciences at university. In theory, a four year natural sciences programme allows a year (on average) for each subject plus a year for some specialization. Taught in an interdisciplinary problem-based way, this provides scope for the coverage of most of the core of the three sciences, and an appreciation of the applications. The final year might integrate discipline specialisation with education, as in the undergraduate programme of Physics with QTS (Qualified Teacher Status). The experience of problem-based tuition will enable these graduates to fill in any gaps in their knowledge, which they will have to do anyway over the course of a career as new discoveries percolate down into the school syllabus.

This then opens the way to a different approach to science education in which it becomes the norm to study Science through school, and in the initial years at university, specializing only later once students have enough knowledge to find their true interests and talents. Readers familiar with the system in Scotland will find this less revolutionary than might be thought. The Scottish (4-year) system lacks only a degree of integration in the first two years of the sciences, and some extension to later years.

We know that most graduates in physics and chemistry do not go on to employments that require much (if any) of their discipline content knowledge. (The same can be said of many other non-vocational university disciplines, which might also benefit from an interdisciplinary core, but let us approach things one Everest at a time.) Such a structure would have the possibility of providing society with the skilled labour required to support the economy, and more rounded and satisfied graduates.

7.5 Personalised curricula

Having laid out a large scale picture for the future landscape, I want to turn to the small scale. What do we want out of education? Do we want to be happy, and if so, what does this mean?

> For our interviewees, meaningfulness, perhaps unsurprisingly, was often associated with a sense of pride and achievement at a *job well done*, whether they were professionals or manual workers. Those who could see that they had *fulfilled their potential*, or who found their work creative, absorbing and interesting, tended to perceive their work as more meaningful than others (my italics) [11].

The key phrase here is the fulfilment of potential, where that potential is for something we consider worthwhile, and that we can do at least as well as anyone else. (I will not be happy if it turns out that someone else has written this (equivalent) book better than I have.) A curriculum is therefore successful when it provides this opportunity for fulfilment. In some cases, fulfilment may come only after graduation, but it would be better if every student had a sense of fulfilled potential as part of their educational experience. Since every student is different, this brings us back to the personalised curriculum.

Students do not know what they need to learn or even, often, what they want to learn. They need to discover this as they progress through the educational system. You might therefore think I would advocate multiple pathways with large option choices. In fact, I think this is too inefficient for a mass system, and focusses on content not skills. In any case, we have already decided that there is a common list of skills and a basic core content. And I explained in section 2.9 how for efficiency I would put optional material within modules. Personalisation here means that all students get to choose something they are good at, or want to try out, in some form of extension work beyond the defined curriculum content.

A second aspect of personalisation comes in the development of skills. Students require widely different amounts of practice to master different skills. Once a student has demonstrated mastery there is no point in further detailed assessment. The time saved can be devoted to providing additional opportunities for other students, who need more practice to work on feedback and improve. By integrating skills and content, and through the happy coincidence that the skills for the workplace are essentially the same as those of the academic researcher, the problem-based approach of the apprentice model supports such personalised curricula. By automating to a large extent the administrative component, technology should make it economically feasible to implement this.

Technology is also enabling when, in conjunction with the personalised curriculum, we consider a personalised assessment profile. Different attributes should not be lumped together in a single module mark for two reasons. First, a single module mark should not be used to disguise weaknesses. Equally importantly it should not hide particular strengths. I would argue that skills and content marks should appear separately, and provide a more complete graduate profile.

7.6 Sustainability

Finally, I want to return to where we started: how can we characterise the role of a modern university? I can scarcely do the subject justice in a page or two, or argue my point with the polemical effulgence of Collini [12] or the eloquent religious conviction of Cardinal Newman [13], but I want to make one observation that differs from these and others: I want to try to justify the view of the university as a place of a liberal education, rather than as a business proposition, in terms of the contemporary zeitgeist.

With evident sarcasm Collini summarises the evolution of universities to the present day thus: 'In the long march that has seen universities function as seminaries, finishing schools, government staff colleges, depositories of culture, nurseries of citizenship and centres of scientific research, they were now to turn themselves into plcs'. Newman's education of the whole person has morphed into the narrow ambition of employability, more accurately described as life skills, and research on mathematics in ancient Sumeria is now to be justified by the impact of this knowledge on the current economy. If there is a better case to be made for the contemporary university than as an ajunct to UK-PLC, we need to make it in terms of widely shared values, without descending into corporate mission statements (cultivate minds, promoting inclusivity, etc). These are meaningless because they are uncontestable (foster bigotry, anyone?). The idea of the university as a place of liberal education was understood seamlessly in the past, because the main role of the institution was to reproduce itself: scholars taught students to become scholars. The present role has expanded to be more like schools, whose main purpose is not to produce school teachers.

We have pointed to the contribution to an educated workforce, the maintenance of social coherence and the underpinning of a functioning democracy, but this is a wish-list rather than the quiddity of the institution. Let us turn the question round: what would we lose if universities were not to exist? According to the current doctrine, we should lose the ability to become richer, to increase GDP. But, as Aristotle pointed out some time ago, to acquire money for its own sake is not a valuable goal. What we actually want is social and economic progress, progress in medicine and technology. In any case, becoming richer with current technology is not sustainable.

So, we are led to the notion of sustainability. Some would say that this is such a vague concept as to be meaningless. I would argue that it is contestable in the same way as are all general ideas, like justice and equality. The fact that such concepts are difficult to pin down does not mean we should ban them from discourse.

Sustainability is about preserving natural and social capital. The maintenance and expansion of social capital is where universities play their unique and crucial role. Teaching the elements of social capital is not just about passing on to the next generation what we know, but passing on the way that we know it. It is therefore about embedding those values in the institutional structure. That is what the university is for. That is what a well-chosen pedagogy helps to achieve. Are problem-based pedagogies the answer to everything? I don't know, but getting education right is certainly the answer to most things.

This book has drawn largely on physics and physics has a large role to play in driving towards a sustainable future. But, sustainability is much wider. Sustainability encompasses environment, economy, equity or social justice as well as science and technology. There is no discipline that does not have a voice in this, whether it is to understand our culture, our relationships with the natural world, our social organisation, or our technical abilities in medicine, materials and information technology. Physics is in a position to contribute to all of these, but above all, with other disciplines alike, to add to the knowledge of the Universe in which our world is worth sustaining.

References

[1] Schuster J H and Finkelstein M J 2007 *On the Brink: Assessing the Status of the American Faculty* (UC Berkeley: Center for Studies in Higher Education) (https://cshe.berkeley.edu/sites/default/files/publications/rop.schuster.3.07.pdf)

[2] Klopper C J and Power B M 2014 The casual approach to teacher education: What effect does casualisation have for Australian university teaching? *Austr. J. Teacher Educ.* **39** (see also https://theconversation.com/casual-academics-arent-going-anywhere-so-what-can-universities-do-to-ensure-learning-isnt-affected-113567)

[3] Kolb D A 1984 *Experiential Learning: Experience as the Source of Learning and Development* (Englewood Cliffs, NJ: Prentice-Hall)

[4] Carroll J B 1963 A model of school learning *Teach. Coll. Rec.* **64** 723–33

[5] De Vos H 1998 Educational effects: a simulation-based analysis *PhD thesis* Universiteit Twente, Netherlands

[6] Scheerens J 1997 Conceptual models and theory embedded principles on effective schooling *School Effect. School Improv. Int. J. Res. Policy Pract.* **8** 269–310
[7] Princeton University (wordnet.princeton.edu/perl/webwn)
[8] Wikipedia (en.wikipedia.org/wiki/Physics)
[9] Institute of Physics (http://www.physics.org/article-questions.asp?id=18)
[10] O'Neill S 2011 Open your mind to interdisciplinary research *New Sci.* **209** 52 (https://www.newscientist.com/article/mg20928002-100-open-your-mind-to-interdisciplinary-research/)
[11] Catherine B and Adrian M 2016 *MIT Sloan Manage. Rev.* **57** (available from Sussex Research Online: http://sro.sussex.ac.uk/61282/)
[12] Collini S 2012 *What Are Universities For?* (London: Penguin Books)
[13] Newman J H 1996 *The Idea of a University* ed F M Turner (New Haven, CT: Yale University Press) (Original edition 1852)

www.ingramcontent.com/pod-product-compliance
Lightning Source LLC
Chambersburg PA
CBHW080552230426
43663CB00015B/2814